LANGUAGE IS THE KEY

LANGUAGE IS THE KEY
The Canadian Language Benchmarks Model

EDITED BY

Monika Jezak

University of Ottawa Press
2017

uOttawa

The University of Ottawa Press gratefully acknowledges the support extended to its publishing list by Canadian Heritage through the Canada Book Fund, by the Canada Council for the Arts, by the Ontario Arts Council, by the Federation for the Humanities and Social Sciences through the Awards to Scholarly Publications Program, and by the University of Ottawa.

Copy editing: Susan James
Proofreading: Robbie McCaw
Typesetting: Counterpunch Inc.
Cover design: Thierry Black and Elizabeth Schwaiger

Library and Archives Canada Cataloguing in Publication

Language is the key : a Canadian Language Benchmarks model / edited by Monika Jezak.

Includes bibliographical references and index.
Issued in print and electronic formats.
ISBN 978-0-7766-2583-6 (softcover). — ISBN 978-0-7766-2584-3 (PDF).-- ISBN 978-0-7766-2585-0 (EPUB). — ISBN 978-0-7766-2586-7 (Kindle)

1. English language — Study and teaching as a second language. 2. French language — Study and teaching as a second language. 3. English language — Study and teaching — Canada. 4. French language — Study and teaching — Canada. 5. Immigrants — Education — Canada. 6. Adult education — Canada. I. Jezak, Monika, 1962–, editor

PE1128.A2L34 2017   428.0071'071   C2017-903655-6
                                                C2017-903656-4

@ Monika Jezak, 2017
under Creative Commons License Attribution —
Non Commercial Share Alike 4.0 International.
(CC BY-NC-SA 4.0)

Table of Contents

Table of Main Acronyms vii

Foreword
Monika Jezak 1

1   Introduction: *Canadian Language Benchmarks* and *Niveaux de compétence linguistique canadiens* – Canadian Language Framework in the Era of Glocalization
Monika Jezak and Enrica Piccardo 7

2   Design-Based Research Methodology for Establishing the Common Theoretical Framework and the CLB/NCLC Scales
Monique Bournot-Trites 31

3   Teaching and Assessment with the CLB: Teacher Experiences and Perspectives
Eve Haque and Antonella Valeo 55

4   Teaching and Assessment: Using the CLB in a Range of Contexts under the Stewardship of the Centre for Canadian Language Benchmarks
Anne Senior 71

5   The NCLC in Minority Settings: Past and Future Projects
Élissa Beaulieu and Morgan Le Thiec 89

6   Conclusion: Building a Bridge to the Future – Potential Contribution of the CLB and the NCLC
Samira ElAtia 107

Contributors 121

Table of Main Acronyms

English

CLB: Canadian Language Benchmarks
CCLB: Centre for Canadian Language Benchmarks
CEFR: Common European Framework of Reference for Languages
ACTFL: American Council for the Teaching of Foreign Languages
CIC (since 2016, IRCC) Citizenship and Immigration Canada / Immigration, Refugees and Citizenship Canada
LINC: Language Instruction for Newcomers to Canada program
TESL: Teachers of English as a Second Language Association

French

NCLC : Niveaux de compétence linguistique canadiens
CNCLC : Centre des Niveaux de compétence linguistique canadiens
EQ : Échelle Québécoise
CLIC : Cours de langue pour les immigrants au Canada

Foreword

Monika Jezak
University of Ottawa

I have been, on numerous occasions, an advisor on the *Niveaux de compétence linguistique canadiens* (NCLC) since 2009, but it was my research residency at the Centre for Canadian Language Benchmarks (CCLB) in the fall of 2015 that really brought home to me the scope, value, and quality of the Benchmarks project. The great efforts involved in the development of the *Canadian Language Benchmarks* (CLB) and the *Niveaux de compétence linguistique canadiens* (NCLC) gave birth to the highly efficient system of official language training that we know today. Indeed, as I was perusing documents related to the French and English standards, and various research papers, I came to realize that this success depended on many factors, namely: twenty years of outstanding, yet understated work by leading Canadian scholars (often not even directly acknowledged in the published documents); a steady commitment by government and non government stakeholders at the federal, provincial, and local levels; and, last but not least, unconditional commitment and caring on the part of an invested community of practice.

Modern Canada has a humanist view of immigrant integration and prides itself on being a welcoming land. As recently as March 6, 2016, during an interview with Lara Logan on the American television program *60 minutes*, Prime Minister Justin Trudeau stated that "accepting 25,000 Syrian refugees does right by the values that define us as a nation," and that "welcoming those immigrants is not just about welcoming 25,000 Syrian refugees, it's welcoming 25,000 new Canadians." These statements fall in line with the last fifty years of Canadian non-discriminatory immigration policy and implicitly underline the importance of immigrant access to official languages: a necessary, even though not sufficient, means to successful integration, as underscored in the CCLB motto: *Language is the key*.

It is towards this humanist goal that generations of Canadian researchers and practitioners have offered their knowledge, expertise, hard work, creativity, and problem-solving ingenuity. This book is a testimony to the journey that led to the present state of Benchmarks-related language training, and a tribute to all those who contributed to the excellence of this Canadian product.

Intended Readership

This book is intended for broad readership. Given the dearth of comprehensive appraisals of the Canadian Benchmark system, it is meant as a basic academic reference for discussion, in the Canadian context, of language policy, linguistic integration of adult migrants, second language teacher education, and task-based language learning. It is relevant to Canadian researchers, graduate and undergraduate students, policy-makers, and various second language training stakeholders (administrators, instructors, assessors, curriculum and teaching material designers, and others). Finally, the book is of relevance internationally as well, in an ongoing reflection in the community of researchers and political decision-makers concerned with similar products abroad, such as the Common European Framework of Reference (CEFR) and the ACTFL guidelines.

Book Structure

The book guides the reader through a reflection on the past, present, and future of the Canadian Benchmarks. It begins with a critical overview of the political and historical context that led to the present international and national positioning of the framework. It continues with its theoretical grounding, and proceeds with a description of current practices, tools, and resources. The conclusion builds on the information provided in preceding chapters to offer an outlook into the framework's future possibilities for growth.

In the introductory chapter, Enrica Piccardo of the University of Toronto, OISE, and I overview the past and present of the Canadian language framework for adult immigrants. We deemed it necessary to re-state the definition and the main features of both the CLB and the NCLC, as well as to trace the historical and the political context that led to the development of these Canadian standards. We stressed also the fact that they do not operate presently in a vacuum: they are indeed a part of a global education market which they share with other language frameworks. We used the concept of "glocalization" to explain the impact of this new dynamic on the positioning of the CLB and the NCLC.

The second chapter is by Monique Bournot-Trites of the University of British Columbia, who was a project lead for the development of the common theoretical framework for both English- and French-language standards. This chapter gives an overview of the CLB- and NCLC-related research. In particular, it outlines a design-based methodology used in various CCLB projects, and sheds light on the meticulous validation process that led to the common theoretical framework and to the scale-building.

The third chapter, by Eve Haque and Antonella Valeo of York University, gives voice to the CLB teachers. Using data gathered through various surveys, the authors reflect on the Benchmarks-related classroom and testing practices, teaching methodologies and contexts, as well as teacher training. They do a critical appraisal of the notion of *continuum of development* and of the *task* as the backbone of teaching in the CLB. Finally, and my personal favourite, the authors draw on the interview material to show how the CLB may inform teachers' everyday classroom practices.

The fourth and the fifth chapters provide an overview of CLB- and NCLC-related materials, tools, and resources for teaching and assessment. The author of chapter four is Anne Senior, while chapter five was written by Élissa Beaulieu and Morgan Le Thiec, the CLB and NCLC specialists respectively. What is striking in comparing the chapters is the concurrent parallelism yet asymmetry of the two linguistic contexts. On the one hand, almost all assessment tools, teaching materials, training programs, and learning support resources, have their equivalent in French and English. On the other hand, the CLB benefit from the majority-language context, with a large number of learners in ESL classes and a multitude of programs, while the NCLC-related teaching is scattered across the country, and altogether inconspicuous. Consequently, the CLB get priority in developing tools and resources, with the French side translating or adapting the existing English material. The same goes for teacher status and training, where a much more robust system was developed on the English side, resulting, over the last twenty years, in a much stronger community of practice, and a nationwide, recognizable, "Benchmarks teaching culture." Clearly, both CLB- and NCLC-related teaching and assessment face challenges for the future and will need nurturing to continue their growth in Canada. However, given the new Canadian demographics where Francophone and Francophile immigration is necessary for the survival of French communities outside of Quebec,[1] the NCLC has yet to gain proper recognition for the crucial role it plays in those particular French minority contexts.

In the concluding chapter, Samira ElAtia offers a bold outlook on the future of the CLB, the NCLC, and the CCLB, proposing various scenarios to branch the Benchmarks out into the domains of higher education, essential skills, literacy, and workplace training, as well as international and indigenous languages. The choice of Samira to write a conclusion was highly symbolic, since she works at an institution loaded with Benchmarks history, the English Language Program of the University of Alberta where Dr. Pawlikowska-Smith drafted a version of the CLB in 2000.

As mentioned before, the chapters in this book are meant to be a tribute to the excellence of Canadian policy, research, and practice in official language training for adult immigrants. The recognition of exceptional achievements does not mean there were no past failures, or present and future challenges. The standardization of official language teaching and assessment (much as it is a salient trait of modern education markets) is an ongoing struggle, and shall be seen, as proposed by Enrica Piccardo, as a "non-finito" process.[2] A "non finito" is a sculpting technique where parts of the sculpture remain as raw stone. In Michelangelo's High Renaissance Italy, the non-finished aspect of the sculpture was perceived as the artists' failure. However, some three hundred years later, another artist, Rodin, prided himself on his non-finitos, making them his artistic trademark. It will be up to the readers to approach the material presented in this book with the eyes of Michelangelo or Rodin.

Enjoy!

Notes

1 Fraser, Graham, and François Boileau. 2014. *Agir maintenant pour l'avenir des communautés francophones : pallier le déséquilibre en immigration.* Ottawa : Ministre des Travaux publics et des Services gouvernementaux Canada. 38 pages.
2 Piccardo, Enrica, 2012. "Le Cadre européen de référence au-delà de l'Europe, un outil confronté à son propre succès. Quelles conséquences possibles ? Quels effets de retour ?" *Symposium Échelles de compétence en langue additionnelle: outils en transition.* ACLA annual conference, Waterloo, Ontario.

CHAPTER 1

Introduction: The *Canadian Language Benchmarks* and *Niveaux de compétence linguistique canadiens* – Canadian Language Framework in the Era of Glocalization

Monika Jezak
University of Ottawa
Enrica Piccardo
University of Toronto, OISE

The twentieth anniversary of the *Canadian Language Benchmarks* (CLB) is an apt occasion to review the origins of the CLB and the *Niveaux de compétence linguistique canadiens* (NCLC), and to consider their current status in official-languages training for adult immigrants in Canada. The chapter begins with a brief definition and description of the two frameworks, follows with their historical and political context, and continues with an outline of the mechanisms at work in the "Canadian model" of language training for adult immigrants. In order to trace the process that led to their development, the CLB and the NCLC are situated in the context of language education in relation to other Canadian and international standards. The final section applies the concept of glocalization as a basis for exploring the position of the various standards in the global–local continuum.

1. Brief Definition and Description of the CLB and the NCLC

Definition
Like other contemporary language standards, the CLB and the NCLC are scales representing all stages of learner language proficiency. These scales were implemented by the federal ministry of immigration for use with adult immigrants.[1] They consist of twelve

benchmarks divided into three levels (beginner, intermediate, and advanced) that cover four language skills (listening and reading comprehension, speaking, and writing). The two frameworks include an explanation of the development of the scales, an outline of the target clientele, a review of the theoretical underpinnings, and guidelines for teaching and assessment. The authors of the CLB and the NCLC state that these documents provide a national standard for French and English programs in various contexts, and a framework for learning, teaching, program planning, and evaluation of second or additional languages in Canada. They further clarify that these documents are not meant to serve as curricula, teaching methodology, or assessment tools (CIC and CCLB 2012a, v; CIC and CCLB 2012b, 1).

Since the publication, twenty years ago, of the first version of the CLB for English as a second language, many related tools for language teaching, learning, and assessment have become available. These resources, as well as a number of language training programs based on the 2012 versions of the CLB and the NCLC, can be found on the dedicated site: http://www.language.ca.

Main features
A unique feature of the CLB and the NCLC is that the two standards are parallel yet distinct; they are not translations of each other. Their application is closely linked to the requirements for settlement of newcomers to Canada (e.g., the recognition of professional qualifications) and for citizenship. Since such requirements are common to both official languages, the description of language proficiency at **each benchmark must be the same in French and in English,** especially in the case of cut levels such as the minimum requirement for granting Canadian citizenship or for admission to professional associations.

The language needs of newcomers and the skills they will require, however, will differ according to whether they choose to settle in an English community or a French minority community. As an example, newcomers who decide to settle in an Anglophone province may self-identify as members of that province's French minority because their language proficiency is stronger in that second language. As a result, their use of the two official languages would be quite different: English in an Anglophone community would be mainly used for activities of daily living, such as finding housing or running errands. In contrast, French in a minority context would more likely be used for social and community services, such as seeking medical attention or helping a child who attends a French-language school. Accordingly, the standards, apart from being equivalent, must offer a wide range of **specific contents and descriptors related to situations that newcomers might face in each of the two official languages.**

Whereas twelve benchmarks might seem excessive in comparison to other frameworks, the highly contextualized nature of the CLB and the NCLC justifies this choice. The **many cut points** on the continuum help Canadian managers assess, with precision, what level adult immigrants have achieved in their linguistic integration into Canadian society, in order to determine whether language training is required for settlement in the host community, whether language resources are needed for seeking employment, whether prior learning in English or French is adequate for the practice of their chosen career, or whether the newcomer is able to pass the citizenship test. The ability to precisely identify the acquired level of proficiency makes possible services tailored to the specific needs of the language learner.

The highly contextualized nature of the CLB and the NCLC, in particular their intended use for newcomers to Canada, explains the strong Canadian character of these two standards, since part of their mission is to convey the brand and values of Canadian identity. Examples of the Canadian ethos abound in the descriptors and language tasks found in both frameworks. The very fact of having two parallel but distinct documents reflects the bilingual nature of the country. The Canadianity[2] of these standards is deeply rooted in the culture and tradition of language training for adult immigrants in Canada, as detailed in what follows.

2. Historical and Political Context: The Development and Implementation of the Canadian System of Training in the Official Languages for Adult Immigrants

Immigration has always played a major role in Canadian history. The federal Immigration Regulations of 1967 introduced a professional and educational merit-point system for admission to Canada. This system led to changes in the law that abolished ethnic and racial discrimination. This in turn led to an ever-increasing proportion of newcomers who belong to a variety of cultural communities (Boyd and Vickers 2000, Li 2000).

The integration and adaptation of immigrants to a host society depends largely on their knowledge of the official languages. The Immigration Regulations, however, generated an increased presence of languages other than French or English. While in the early twentieth century, 93 percent of the Canadian population had either English or French as their first language, the years from 1950 to 1970 show an increase in the number of native speakers of other European languages such as German, Italian, Dutch, and Ukrainian. Since the 1970s, there has been an influx of speakers of non-European languages. For example, the number of native speakers of Indo-Pakistani languages rose from 33,000 in 1971 to 900,000 in 2006. Over a century, the allophone[3] proportion of the Canadian population rose from 7 percent to nearly 20 percent. By 2011, 6.6 million people reported using a language other than French or English at home (Lachapelle and Lepage 2010, Statistics Canada 2012).

The ethnic diversification of the 1970s and 1980s created a greater need for language training, which in turn led to an increase in the number of language programs available to adult immigrants, particularly in areas directly affected by the tide of immigration. During this period, co-ordination of services among local administrations and community organizations responsible for language training was not entirely adequate, not only at the level of curriculum and certification, but also in relation to teaching qualifications. Measures intended to co-ordinate language services, however, soon began to emerge, as shown below.

Shortly after the adoption of the new Immigration Regulations in 1967, two major pieces of federal legislation begin to define Canadian identity: the *Official Languages Act* of 1969 and the *Multiculturalism Act* of 1971.

The *Official Languages Act* (along with the later *Constitution Act* of 1982, which opens with the *Canadian Charter of Rights and Freedoms*) defines official bilingualism. It establishes institutional bilingualism by promoting equality of status and equal rights and privileges (point 16.1) for Francophone and Anglophone Canadians. As Leclerc (2010, 76) underlines, "Canada isn't officially bilingual, only the federal state is. The provinces, municipalities, private organizations (and individuals) are not directly affected by Canada's institutional bilingualism."

By instituting an Anglophone-Francophone duality, however, the legislation **removes from the national debate all language matters related to allophone immigration**, whether the study of English or French, or language planning for immigration languages. A striking result of this language policy is the emergence of a "third force" in an increasingly multilingual Canada, outside the sphere of the languages of the "founding peoples," (Commission on Bilingualism and Biculturalism, cited in Li 2000, 1). In line with this, Burnaby (2008, 336) observes: "Reading official statements, one would scarcely believe that Canadians speak languages other than English and French. Federal statements carefully refer to speakers of non-official languages as other 'cultural' groups."

The Canadian policy on multiculturalism becomes the government's response to the growing ethnic diversity. On the subject of the study of official languages, policy states that the government will continue to help immigrants to acquire at least one of the two official languages and to integrate into Canadian society (Government of Canada 1971, 8546). Both the *Immigration Act* of 1976 and the *Multiculturalism Act* of 1988 reaffirm these commitments. The latter, in points 3 (i) and (j), highlights the status of official languages along with the promotion of multiculturalism in keeping with the national commitments to the two official languages.

It is through social policy related to immigration and multiculturalism that the federal, provincial, and local governments address allophone language planning, including issues related to the teaching of official languages to adult immigrants. This approach has a number of practical implications.

First, **the structure and content of language courses is subject to immigration-policy priorities**. Since 1970s, these priorities have concerned – to varying degrees depending on the period – the economy (for example, access to the labour force) and social cohesion (for example, citizen participation) (Williams 1998).

An added feature of the Canadian system is that official-language education comes under provincial and local jurisdictions, whereas issues related to immigration, multiculturalism, and citizenship (including issues related to the official languages for adult immigrants) fall under various federal, provincial, and local authorities. This structure results in **shared and negotiated responsibility in matters related to language training,** which certain authors refer to as "diffuse decision making" (Churchill 2011). This type of governance sometimes makes it difficult to identify by whom and how policies are introduced, approved, financed, and implemented.

Diffuse decision making, while facilitating the negotiation, compromise, and democratic dialogue characteristic of Canadian policy-making (Cardinal 2015), gave rise in 1970s and 1980s to a great diversity of programs across the nation. For example, certain school boards in charge of language training for adult immigrants, such as the Toronto boards, adopted innovative methods following a massive influx of immigrants from diverse backgrounds. Meanwhile, other service providers with limited resources added few changes to teaching materials or curriculum development (Fleming 2007). In this context, language training centres for adult immigrants across the country expressed the need for a national standard for all language programs.

In the decades of the 1970s and 1980s, pioneer initiatives of the "Canadian Model" for immigrant language training were introduced by the federal government in programs such as the Canadian Job Strategies Program (CJS) (1978) or the Settlement Language Training Program (SLTP) (1986). The first example, the CJS program, was directly linked to employment, and the SLTP program was linked to settlement policy. These examples clearly illustrate the reference made above to a direct connection between social policy and language training for adult immigrants.

Some aspects of the diffuse decision-making process were even adopted by existing second-language training structures, such as the shared responsibility between the federal and provincial governments, whereby the provincial government took charge of program delivery (staffing teachers, selecting teaching materials), while the federal government handled the selection and financial support of participants.

3. A New Phase: The Impact of Canada's 1990–1995 Program and the Development of Language Standards

The five-year immigration program that ran from 1990 to 1995 opened new opportunities for immigrants with marketable skills or financial resources. It also promoted a harmonization of federal and provincial immigration policy that prioritized language training, since knowledge of one or both official languages was seen as crucial for the modern workplace (Burnaby 1998). Despite the recession of the

1990s, Canada hosted an unprecedented number of highly educated immigrants or investors from Asia and Africa for whom neither French nor English was their mother tongue.

In 1991, encouraged by the call for better co-ordination of federal and provincial immigration policies, Quebec negotiated with the federal government to take full responsibility provincially for selection of immigrants, settlement services, and language training. The result was a distinct system of language training for adult immigrants in Quebec. The province also developed its own language standard: *L'Échelle québécoise des niveaux de compétence en français des personnes immigrantes adultes* (Government of Quebec 2011), discussed further on in this chapter.

As for the other provinces and territories, in 1991 the federal government's Ministry of Employment and Immigration set up an advisory board made up of immigration stakeholders to assess the language training needs of adult immigrants. Following extensive nationwide consultation with teachers, students, program administrators, and others in the field, the advisory board submitted a number of key recommendations to policy makers:

1. Better co-ordination among service providers;
2. Establishment of a common standard for teacher training;
3. Standardization of tests and certification procedures;
4. Development of a national curriculum;
5. A package of measures for program delivery, including an increase in the amount of government-funded training and a reduction in class size.

These nationwide consultations also served to highlight the need for nationally recognized language standards.

The CLB and the NCLC in a historical perspective: origins and development

In 1993, the federal Ministry of Citizenship and Immigration followed through by setting up a national advisory group to develop a language-standards framework and provide support to the group's editorial team. *Canadian Language Benchmarks: English as a second language for adults, English as a second language for literacy learners (working document)* was first published in 1996 (CIC 1996), and has since become the basis of program design, teaching methodology, materials development, and assessment in English as a second language. The Benchmarks were field-tested, revised, and published in the definitive version in 2000 (Pawlikowska-Smith 2000). Their counterpart for French as a second language, the *Niveaux de compétence linguistique canadiens* (NCLC) was first published in 2002 under the working title *Standards linguistiques canadiens 2002: français langue seconde pour adultes* (CIC and CCLB 2002), and in the definitive version in 2006 (CIC and CCLB 2006). Ever since, the CLB/NCLC have played a unifying role in official-languages teaching and assessment practices for adult immigrants in Canada.

As a follow-up in 1998, a national administrative body was created to independently direct the implementation of these new language standards: the Centre for Canadian Language Benchmarks (CCLB).

The CCLB's mandate is to implement the CLB and the NCLC in a range of English and French as a second language programs and assessment structures across the country. It hosts the two standards, advocates their use, and oversees their updates. It fosters excellence in official language teaching to adult immigrants and provides support for program administration. It also provides strategic direction for the education sector, for access to the labour market, and for the integration of immigrants. It is also responsible for quality assurance of products based on the two standards. The CCLB is governed by a Board of Directors made up of representatives from organizations and interest groups, and a network of experts and practitioners in French and English as a second language from across the country. Because the mandate of the Centre cuts across several sectors and jurisdictions, it works in close collaboration with all Canadian sectors involved in the teaching of official languages to adult immigrants: federal ministries of Citizenship and Immigration and Human Resources and Skills Development, various provincial government ministries, and school boards and colleges, as well as professional associations such as TESL Canada (http://www.tesl.ca/).

In 2009, as reported in the preface to the 2012 versions of the CLB and the NCLC, with funding support from the federal and some provincial governments, the CCLB "embarked on a national consultation to determine how the CLB and the NCLC should evolve to meet the changing needs of stakeholders. More than 1,300 people, representing multiple stakeholders, participated in the process" (CIC 2012b, I).

Following this initial consultation, a series of forums were held, involving stakeholders in the field of immigrant language training and experts in the field of second languages in Canada. Their objective was to ensure that the revised CLB and NCLC standards had the rigour and validity required for use in a broad range of contexts. These forums also provided a list of practical recommendations for updating the Benchmarks, such as improving descriptors for proficiency levels, bridging gaps noted in the NCLC continuum, and adding examples of suitable tasks for work or study contexts.

After years of work by specialists, a common theoretical framework for the two standards was completed (Bournot-Trites et al. 2015), followed up by two substantially redesigned frameworks, the CLB 2012 and the NCLC 2012. The official summary states:

> Those documents draw upon widely accepted research in the field of language education, including key principles applicable to all languages and contributions from the ESL and FSL fields. The theoretical framework underwent extensive independent review at each stage of its development. It was later compared with the Common European Framework of Reference (CEFR), the American Council for the Teaching of Foreign Languages (ACTFL) guidelines, and the Échelle québécoise. These comparisons showed that the theoretical framework was consistent not only with the theoretical concepts it articulated, but also with the key principles underlying other language frameworks. The CLB and the NCLC were then validated against the theoretical framework to determine whether they accurately reflected the underlying theory. ... The documents were further fine-tuned and both have been accepted as accurate reflections of the theoretical framework and consistent with widely accepted research. (Citizenship and Immigration Canada 2012a, II)

L'Échelle québécoise des niveaux de compétence en français des personnes immigrantes adultes

As mentioned earlier, the NCLC are not the only standard for evaluating French-language proficiency in Canada. Whereas the NCLC are a federal standard, another standard was developed specifically for the province of Quebec: *L'Échelle québécoise des niveaux de compétence en français des personnes immigrantes adultes* (Government of Quebec 2011).

L'*Échelle québécoise* is a descriptive framework for language proficiency similar to the CLB/NCLC. It also divides proficiency into four skills (listening, reading, speaking, and writing), three stages of development, and twelve benchmarks, and is intended for adult immigrants. This standard, however,

> stems from the Quebec government's political will to harmonize francization services for immigrants through schools and community organizations who partner with the Ministère de l'Immigration et des Communautés culturelles (MICC), and school boards under the Ministère de l'Éducation, du Loisir et du Sport du Québec (MELS). ... This standard, which includes l'Échelle québécoise des niveaux de compétence en français des personnes immigrantes adultes and the Programme-cadre de français pour les personnes immigrantes adultes au Québec, is also used by ministries and organizations such as l'Office québécois de la langue française (OQLF) and le ministère de l'Emploi et de la Solidarité sociale (MESS) to measure the French language competence of their clientele. (Government of Quebec 2011, 4)

A special case of language-proficiency description in Canada: Qualification Standards in Relation to Official Languages for Federal Employees

This section will end with a description of a standard of a very different nature: the *Qualification Standards in Relation to Official Languages for Federal Employees* (the *Standards*). Created in 1984, these were the very first Canadian language standards. According to Gale and Slivinski (1988, 84), they apply to all federal government positions requiring the use of both official languages, and their scope is very broad, concerning: "approximately one-quarter of a million employees ... distributed nation-wide throughout approximately sixty government departments and agencies and seventy-five different occupational groups."

The *Standards* are governed as much by public policy (*Public Service Employment Act*, *Financial Administration Act*), as by language policy (the *Official Languages Act*, the *Policy on Official Languages for Human Resources Management*, the *Directive on the Staffing of Bilingual Positions*, and the *Directive on the Linguistic Identification of Positions or*

Functions) (Treasury Board of Canada Secretariat 2015). Briefly, the *Standards* are a description of the language requirements for positions that involve communication with the public, service delivery, and for the language of work. They divide the language-proficiency continuum into three skills (reading comprehension, writing, and speaking), and include two categories of language proficiency for bilingual positions: general skills (with three levels of requirements according to position: A for minimum requirements, B for intermediate, and C for advanced), and specialized skills (requiring code P).

4. Canada and Other Standards: the Common European Framework of Reference for Languages (CEFR)

Europe, the birthplace of the *Common European Framework of Reference for Languages* (CEFR) (Council of Europe 2001), has a long tradition of the co-existence of languages, the teaching of foreign languages, and the creating of links between research and practice in language teaching (for example, the International Association of Applied Linguistics was founded in 1969, and the Centre de recherche et d'étude pour la diffusion du français in 1959). It also has a long tradition of user-centred learning objectives linked to the context of use. The classic case of this is the 1970s *Threshold Level*, which is the precursor of the CEFR, adapted to some thirty languages.

The linking of research, language policy, and foreign-language teaching practices is a central concern for many European member states. The idea of an organization able to accomplish such a mission has held sway in Europe for over half a century.

In fact, foreign-language teaching has been aligned with the educational policies of the Council of Europe since the *European Cultural Convention* of 1954 (Council of Europe 1954). As such, it is subject to the imperatives of human rights, linguistic diversity, and the search for social cohesion: "Language teaching is not only a matter of pedagogy, it is a crucial area for language policy and living together in a democracy" (Council of Europe 2014, 6). The Language Policy Unit of the Council of Europe (supported since 1994 by the European Centre for Modern Languages) plays a central role in the establishment and implementation of language-education policy, and in theoretical reflection on linguistic diversity. Given the sovereignty of member states in the field of education, the Council of Europe exerts only indirect influence, by providing reference documents, guidelines, and instruments (such as the CEFR) on which to base curricula, assessment, and national teaching materials.

Policy decisions related to the teaching of foreign languages are traditionally research-based, as in the example of *Threshold Level*. This culture of research gave rise to a range of varied yet complementary events (symposia, colloquia, government research publications, commissions, working groups, and more), culminating in the creation of the CEFR. The levels and descriptors used in the CEFR were developed and validated in a Swiss research project (1993–1996) that used both quantitative and qualitative methods (North 2000, North 2014, North and Schneider 1998). The CEFR is, moreover, increasingly recognized as both a policy standard and the product of advanced research in language teaching and assessment.

The CEFR merging of research and assessment practices would become one of the hallmarks of the "European model." For instance, the *Manual for Relating Language Examinations to the CEFR* (Council of Europe 2009) reports on and models the research required to establish a reliable relationship between examination results and the CEFR levels.

Six levels (grouped into three macro-levels: A1/A2, B1/B2, C1/C2) describe the continuum of language proficiency in the CEFR. The descriptors are positively formulated definitions of the language activities (comprehension, production, interaction, and mediation[4]), which take place in written or oral mode, and of aspects of the competences needed for real-world tasks. As stated by Piccardo (2014, 7), "the main objective of the CEFR is to provide a common language for professionals in the field of language learning and teaching at all levels, to help them in their practice and in achieving their respective goals."

Of special interest here is the relevance of the CEFR for adult migrant language training and assessment, since the majority of European states require proof of competence in the language of the host nation for citizenship, residence, or work permits. In this context, the CEFR provides clear level descriptors rooted in real life that prove essential for the training and assessment of the migrant population. The individual European states, and in general any institution involved in training migrants, could benefit from this contribution.

To support the EU's language policy for adult immigrants, the project Linguistic Integration of Adult Migrants (LIAM) (co-ordinated by researchers and stakeholders in language training and assessment of migrants across Europe) was set up in 2006. The LIAM project, with its focus on migrant needs for linguistic and cultural integration, developed and implemented the CEFR vision of plurilingualism and linguistic diversity, while maintaining the integrity of the levels clearly defined by the CEFR. Hence, LIAM motivates member states to develop competence profiles rather than restricting themselves to assigning levels.

Over time, this approach is intended to raise awareness of the relationship between written standards (such as the CEFR) and the reality on the ground for formal and informal learning or for participation in social life.

5. The CLB and the NCLC in the Context of Language Education: Glocal Perspectives

The glocalization of educational markets

As several authors point out, one of the main features of current educational environments (Canada included) is that they are subject to both local demands (protection of interests of national and local cultures, defining identities, and so on) and global ones (student mobility, transfer of expertise and technologies, access to information on a global scale through new technologies, need for internationally recognized certifications, and more). The co-existence of local and global dynamics is known as glocalization (Ball, Goodson and Maguire 2007; Drori, Höllerer and Walgenbach 2013; Giulianotti and Robertson 2012; Meyrowitz 2005; Ritzer and Ritzer 2012; Rizvi and Lingard 2010). Roudometof (2015, 9) uses a wave analogy to explain this concept:

> In the case of the globalization of X, what actually takes place is the migration and spread of X into different localities. If one further views these localities as having varying degrees of density or "thickness," or to put it differently, as having different wave resistance capacities, the process can then operate in two different ways. First, the wave-like properties can be absorbed and amplified by the local and then reflected back onto the world stage. ... Second, it is possible for a wave to pass through the local and to be refracted by it. ... The local is not annihilated or absorbed or destroyed by globalization but, rather, operates symbiotically with globalization and shapes the end state or result.

The processes of glocalization also apply to language standards. One of the CEFR authors, Brian North, emphasizes that there is no contradiction between the need for a globalizing common standard on the one hand, and the need for local strategies and instruments targeting the specific needs of learners on the other. More specifically, he states (North 2008, 226):

> The aim of a meta-system at a national or international level ought to be to facilitate reflection, communication and networking. The aim of any local strategies ought to be to meet needs in context. The key to linking the two into a coherent system is flexibility: an expandable/contractible descriptive approach in which levels, categories and descriptors can be merged or subdivided in a common hierarchical structure.

The following sections will apply three axes of analysis to investigate the glocal value of the CLB and the NCLC relative to other instruments discussed in this chapter, namely the two other Canadian standards and the CEFR. The three axes are: general versus specific content, easily modified versus less easily modified framework, and bottom-up versus top-down development and implementation.

Positioning the CLB and the NCLC in the global-glocal dynamic

The CLB and the NCLC are not exempt from the influences of this new dynamic in the language teaching, learning, and assessment market that evolves between the demands of globalization and glocalization.

The target clientele of the two Canadian standards is generally made up of mobile adult immigrants seeking recognition of language proficiency acquired abroad or in other parts of Canada. Such recognition implies correlation to other standards.

There are multiple ways to achieve this goal. As discussed at the beginning of this chapter, the CLB and the NCLC, like all other standards, are scales used to describe the continuum of language competence from beginner to advanced levels. Although the cut-points between levels may vary from one standard to another,[5] all have three stages of learning in common: for example, the A levels of the CEFR (basic user) correspond to the beginner stage of the CLB/NCLC, the B levels (independent user) correspond to intermediate, and the C levels (proficient user) correspond to advanced level.

Similarly, the conception of the continuum of language competence (along with the communicative activities in which it is embedded) is at the core of the different standards. The concept of language competence is defined in a comparable if not identical manner. This common ground gives rise to a sort of global common language. The CLB/NCLC converge with the other standards in other ways as well. For example, all contemporary standards view the teaching, learning, and evaluation of language competence holistically, thus closely tied to curriculum design, testing, and teaching materials. The learner-centred approach is another common thread. Lastly, all standards, including the CLB/NCLC, currently favour an action-oriented approach to language teaching. The emphasis is on the performance of language tasks rather than the knowledge of language, and communicative competence is contextualized according to the learner's life experience.

The parallel development of the CEFR and the CLB is significant. The dates of origin, development, and publication are nearly simultaneous (both projects took place between approximately 1995 and 2001, with the respective first versions published in 1996). This parallel process might explain why there was no knowledge transfer between the two projects (although, for example, a major research of all existing assessment instruments was undertaken in preparation for the CEFR); however, it also demonstrates the felt need for clear and transparent language-assessment instruments that could address growing societal needs generated by mobility on both sides of the Atlantic.

In 2008, the Council of Ministers of Education Canada proposed that second or additional language curricula in primary and secondary schools be based on the CEFR (Council of Ministers of Education Canada 2010). Although no one can ascertain the exact number of students of second and additional languages trained and assessed by the "CEFR system," it is safe to say that it is a large number. Second-language instruction in many provinces is mandatory for four or five years; there are also programs such as early French immersion, in which language instruction begins at a very early age. After eight years of use, it is still difficult to assess the exact impact of having second-language programs aligned with the CEFR. Nevertheless, its adoption by the school system is not without impact for the CLB/NCLC, if only because immigrant parents are part of the CLB/NCLC target clientele.

Local, National, and Global Instruments: Features and Roles

As mentioned earlier, the CLB and the NCLC belong to the globalization of education movement by virtue of adopting a conceptual framework and language common to other contemporary standards. However, these standards are also influenced by local factors (dependent on requirements for integration into society), and, in our judgment, their true value is determined in relation to the balance achieved between global and local pressures. Accordingly, content can be more generic when it needs to follow global requirements, but more specific to user context when it must meet mainly local criteria. The framework could be more easily modified and updated when subject to local policy, and less easily modified when global policies take precedent. Similarly, the standards would be developed and implemented using a more top-down approach to suit a global perspective, and a more bottom-up approach for a local one. An analysis follows of the standards introduced above, beginning with those produced for Canada.

L'Échelle québécoise has a **local focus** tied to francization policy for adults in Quebec (hence deals with only one language and is geographically defined). Since it derives directly from provincial immigration policy, *L'Échelle québécoise* must be **modifiable** in line with any major changes to this policy. It was developed with both a **top-down and bottom-up approach at the same time.** Although the process was initiated by the government, the teaching community in charge of the francization of adult immigrants participated throughout the development of this instrument by validating content and providing feedback on its successive versions.

Both the CLB/NCLC and *L'Échelle québécoise* share the clearly similar goals of serving the needs of those engaged in the training and language competence assessment of adult immigrants. It is indisputable, however, that the political choice of developing two distinct instruments reduces *de facto* the potential impact of a single national standard with regard to transparency and ease of implementation, especially for inter-regional mobility. However, these potential disadvantages were taken into account and considerably mitigated *a fortiori* by updating the CLB/NCLC in comparison with other current standards. Aside from these considerations, what is relevant at this point is the challenge of finding a balance between the global goals of these standards and the influence of particularistic interests or claims. The issue at hand is the harmonizing of global and local dimensions in a way that allows enough flexibility to meet specific needs.

The *Standards*, as detailed earlier, define language requirements for specific administrative positions where language, in this case the two official languages, plays a key role in the relationship between institutions and citizens. In contrast, the CLB/NCLC, *L'Échelle québécoise*, and the CEFR focus on learner progress in language competence. Still, the very existence of the *Standards* demonstrates a long-standing goal of developing standards for national comparison, which is a globalizing tendency. At the same time, the *Standards* are linked to a specific work environment, **a local focus. Their specific contents** are directly linked to language tasks required in different positions within the federal public service. These contents must be **easily modified** whenever new language requirement are identified for the positions, or in case of a policy change affecting language use in the workplace. (The latest version was released in 2015.) Given that the *Standards* arise out of federal policy related to management of the public service, with the goal of establishing employee language competence qualifications, their development and implementation are essentially **top-down**.

The CEFR is a standard with a **European focus, but a global scope** (Piccardo, Germain-Rutherford and Clement 2011; Byram and Parmenter 2012). It aims to serve as an extra-national guide for curricula and assessment, suited to European member states, but also relevant outside Europe. **Its contents (descriptions of levels of proficiency, lists of descriptors, and so on) are generic enough to allow substantial adaptation for local use.**

At the same time, as it is rooted in the key values of the European project (the search for social cohesion through cultural exchange, plurilingualism, and so on), **it remains a document of a political nature generated by the context in which it was created.** The 2001 version is still in effect, although a recent major international project is updating the descriptors (North and Panthier 2016 forthcoming, North and Docherty 2016 forthcoming). A series of related tools (guides, textbooks, exemplars of oral and written production aligned with the CEFR levels) are available on-line at the Council of Europe website. The various European language portfolios, with descriptors adapted from those of the CEFR, have their own dedicated websites. Also available on the site of the

European Centre for Modern Languages (ECML) is a wide range of research publications inspired by the CEFR or its derivatives. The ECML is an institution of the Council of Europe; its mission is to implement language policy. Lastly, as the CEFR project is guided by a European body, **a top-down approach in its creation** is implicit. A team of researchers mandated by the Council of Europe developed an instrument that was field-tested through the national education departments and agencies in charge of curricula and assessment. Since its beginnings, the implementation of the CEFR at the local level has posed the greatest challenge, particularly with regard to language teaching itself, and in the provision of evidence to demonstrate a reliable relationship between on the one hand the local objectives, curricula, and examinations, and on the other hand the CEFR levels. This shows how difficult it is to achieve a balance between local and global goals (Martyniuk and Noyons 2006, Broek and van den Ende 2013).

So, how does one situate the CLB/NCLC in this complex landscape, which is currently undergoing major socio-economic shifts? What is the place of the CLB and the NCLC in language training in Canada? Considering their target clientele (adult immigrants integrating into Canadian society), the focus of these two standards seems **both local and global**. Actually, this target clientele has particular language needs: besides the broader needs dictated by the host society, there are the specific needs of the particular community they are joining. Recent immigrants are mobile, both geographically (potentially to other regions in Canada) and socially (vis-à-vis employment or a new role in society). Given this reality, the CLB/NCLC language certifications have to be recognized by all immigrant services across Canada, including Quebec. However, since Quebec adopted its own standard, the CLB/NCLC may find itself at odds with the decisions taken in this particular context, with the possible result that their global role may be called into question. Furthermore, although Quebec immigration policy differs from that of the rest of Canada, citizenship policies are common, implying some commonality between *L'Échelle Québécoise* and the NCLC. Similarly, immigrants, once established and no longer receiving special services for newcomers, are likely to compare their language proficiency to that of native-born Canadians trained in the CEFR system. It follows then that the CLB/NCLC should also be comparable to other certifications, such as those reporting a CEFR level that immigrants from Europe or other countries may have. These examples illustrate the complexity of the context in which the CLB/NCLC are used, where both local and global pressures are equally exerted.

The contents of the CLB/NCLC are relatively specific in order to meet the language needs of newcomers to Canada in their work, study, and life in the community. In this respect, the CLB and the NCLC differ somewhat, to reflect the difference in language use between a majority (English) and minority (French) context. Apart from purely pragmatic language content dealing with living in the host community, searching for work, the practice of a profession, or civic participation, both standards include an introduction to Canadian values and identity. These contents are a unique feature of the two Canadian standards deemed necessary for immigrants wishing to integrate into their new country.

The CLB/NCLC are directly linked to Canadian citizenship and immigration policy, and are **modifiable** in the event of changes to these policies or to the context of language teaching and assessment for adult immigrants, as already mentioned.

Finally, the standards were **developed mainly through a top-down, but also a bottom-up dynamic.** On one hand, immigration, multiculturalism, and citizenship policy, along with federal funding, were crucial to the development and implementation of the CLB and the NCLC. Moreover, the development of the common theoretical framework was research-driven. On the other hand, as mentioned earlier, national consultations and the needs expressed by stakeholders provided the impetus for the updates to the standards. Similarly, the community of practitioners in the field took part in all stages of their development. Finally, the CLB/NCLC initial development process, as well as its updates, were an opportunity for professional development and gave rise to a coherent community of practice, committed to a recognisable CLB/NCLC culture, despite the size of the country and the wide diversity of immigrant language services.

6. Not to Conclude: the CLB/NCLC and the Glocalization Movement

These analyses are not meant to provide a rigid classification, a task beyond our scope. The various facets and implications discussed above clearly demonstrate that such a classification would be unrealistic, and in the long run not very productive. What we do propose are avenues for exploring the implications and consequences of institutional choices at both the local and global levels. A case in point here is the effort made in the European context to overcome particularistic interests and linguistic and cultural differences in order to arrive at a common system that can transcend the local dimension, while remaining open to local adaptation (North 2016, personal communication). In the Canadian context, this endeavour was complicated, at least at the level of implementation, by the presence of strong local dynamics. It should be noted, however, that the idea of providing a more global instrument, less sensitive to local demands, such as the CEFR, requires considerable rigour in the calibration of descriptors, which on one the hand ensures good transferability, but on the other hand hinders the ease of modification. By contrast, an instrument more sensitive to local demands, such as the CLB/NCLC, calls for less rigour in the validation of descriptors, since in any case it will likely require more frequent updates. This less rigorous process of revision offers greater flexibility in exchange. Clearly, glocalization has a powerful impact on all standardization instruments: what matters is an awareness of the possible impact of the choices made.

The aim of this chapter was to describe the CLB and the NCLC and to provide a brief outline of the issues involved, both from a historical perspective and in relation to the current Canadian socio-political context. The two standards were situated within the context of language training for adult immigrants, setting the stage for subsequent chapters which deal with more specific issues: the research dimension of the two standards, the teaching culture they have engendered, and an overview of related practices and resources.

References

Ball, Stephen J., Ivor F. Goodson and Meg Maguire, eds. 2007. *Education, globalization and new times*. London: Routledge.

Bournot-Trites, Monique, Ross Barbour, Monika Jezak, Gail Stewart and Daphné Blouin Carbonneau. 2015. *Theoretical Framework for the Canadian Language Benchmarks and Niveaux de competence linguistique canadiens*. Ottawa: Centre for Canadian Language Benchmarks.

Boyd, Monica, and Michael Vickers. 2000. "100 Years of Immigration in Canada." *Canadian social trends* (5)4: 2–12. Ottawa: Statistics Canada – Catalogue No. 11-008.

Broek, Simon, and Inge van den Ende. 2013. *The Implementation of the Common European Framework for Languages in European Education Systems*. Brussels: Policy Department B: Structural and Cohesion Policies, European Parliament.

Burnaby, Barbara. 1998. "ESL Policy in Canada and the United States: Basis for comparison." In *Language and Politics in the United States and Canada: Myths and Realities* edited by Tom Ricento, and Barbara Burnaby, 243–267. Mahwah, N.J.: Lawrence Erlbaum.

———. 2008. "Language Policy and Education in Canada." In *Encyclopedia of language and education*. 2nd Edition. Volume 1: *Language Policy and Political Issues in Education*, edited by Stephen May and Nancy Hornberger, 331–342. New York: Springer Science + Business Media LLC.

Byram, Michael, and Lynne Parmenter, eds. 2012. *The Common European Framework of Reference. The Globalisation of Language Policy*. Bristol – Buffalo – Toronto: Multilingual Matters.

Cardinal, Linda. 2015. "State tradition and language regime in Canada." In *State Traditions and Language Regimes*, edited by Linda Cardinal and Selma Sonntag, 29–43. Montreal and Kingston: McGill-Queens University Press.

Centre for Canadian Language Benchmarks. 2016. Accessed February 27, 2016. http://www.language.ca.

Churchill, Stacy. 2011. "Redefining language policy as a discipline." *OLBI Working Papers* 3:63–67.

Citizenship and Immigration Canada. 1996. *Canadian Language Benchmarks: English as a Second Language for Adults. English as a second language for literacy learners (working document)*. Ottawa: Minister of Supply and Services Canada.

Citizenship and Immigration Canada, and Centre for Canadian Language Benchmarks. 2002. *Standards linguistiques canadiens 2002: français langue seconde pour adultes*. Ottawa: Minister of Public Works and Services Canada.

———. 2006. *Niveaux de compétence linguistique canadiens 2006: français langue seconde pour adultes*. Ottawa: Citizenship and Immigration Canada.

———. 2012a. *Canadian Language Benchmarks: English as a Second Language for Adults*. Ottawa: Citizenship and Immigration Canada.

———. 2012b. *Niveaux de compétence linguistique canadiens: français langue seconde pour adultes*. Ottawa: Citizenship and Immigration Canada.

Council of Europe. 1954. Convention culturelle européenne. *Série des traités européens - n° 18*. Accessed February 27, 2016. http://www.coe.int/en/web/conventions/full-list/-/conventions/rms/090000168006458c.

———. 2001. *Common European Framework of Reference for Languages: Learning, Teaching, Assessment*. Strasbourg: Language Policy Unit.

———. 2009. *Manuel pour relier les examens au CECR*. Strasbourg: Council of Europe.

———. 2014. *Languages for democracy and social cohesion. Diversity, equity and quality. Sixty years of European co-operation*. Strasbourg: Language Policy Unit.

Council of Ministers of Education Canada. 2010. *L'exploitation du Cadre européen commun de référence pour les langues (CECR) dans le contexte canadien. Guide à l'intention des responsables de l'élaboration des politiques et des concepteurs de programmes d'études*. Ottawa: Council of Ministers of Education Canada.

Drori, Gili S., Markus A. Höllerer, and Peter Walgenbach, eds. 2013. *Global Themes and Local Variations in Organization and Management: Perspectives on Glocalization*. London: Routledge.

Fleming, Douglas. 2007. "Adult immigrant ESL programs in Canada: Emerging trends in the contexts of history, economics and identity." In *The international handbook of English language teaching*, edited by Jim Cummins and Chris Davison, 181–194. New York: Springer.

Gale, Cheryl, and Len Slivinski. 1988. "I/O Psychology in the Canadian Federal Government: The Personnel Psychology Centre of the Public Service Commission." *Canadian Psychology / Psychologie canadienne* 29(1): 84–93.

Giulianotti, Richard, and Roland Robertson. 2012. "Glocalization." In *The Wiley-Blackwell Encyclopedia of Globalization*, edited by George Ritzer. Oxford: Wiley-Blackwell. doi: 10.1002/9780470670590.wbeog254.

Government of Canada. 1967. *Immigration Regulations*. Archives Canada. "Immigration Act, Immigration Regulations, Part 1, amended." RG2-A-1-a, volume 2380, PC1967-1616, August 16 1967. Accessed December 20, 2015. http://www.quai21.ca/recherche/histoire-d-immigration/reglement-sur-l-immigration-decret-du-conseil-cp-1967-1616-1967.

———. 1969. *Official Languages Act*. Archives Canada. Ottawa: SRC 0-2. Accessed December 20, 2015. http://www.axl.cefan.ulaval.ca/amnord/cnd-loi-languesofficielles1969.htm.

———. 1971. *Canada Multiculturalism Act*. Archives Canada. Canada. Parliament. House of Commons. Debates, 1071, volume 115 (187), 28ᵉ Parliament, 3ᵉ Session, tome 8: 8545-8548, Appendix, 8580-8585. Accessed December 20, 2015. http://www.quai21.ca/recherche/histoire-d-immigration/la-politique-canadienne-du-multiculturalisme-de-1971.

———. 1976. *Immigration Act*. Archives Canada. Ottawa: S.C. 25-26. Accessed December 20, 2015. http://www.quai21.ca/recherche/histoire-d-immigration/loi-sur-l-immigration-de-1976.

———. 1982. *Constitution Act*. Accessed December 20, 2015. http://laws-lois.justice.gc.ca/fra/const/page-15.html#h-38.

———. 1988. *Canadian Multiculturalism Act*. Ottawa: S.R.C. 24 (4e suppl.). Accessed December 20, 2015. http://laws-lois.justice.gc.ca/PDF/C-18.7.pdf.

Government of Quebec. 2011. *Échelle québécoise des niveaux de compétence en français des personnes immigrantes adultes*. Montréal: Ministère de l'Immigration et des Communautés culturelles.

Lachapelle, Réjean, and Jean-François Lepage. 2010. *Languages in Canada: 2006 Census*. Ottawa: Statistics Canada – Canadian Heritage.

Leclerc, Jean. 2010. "Les législations linguistiques en Amérique du Nord." *Téléscope* 16 (3): 75–93.

Li, Peter. 2000. *Cultural Diversity in Canada: The Social Construction of Racial Differences*. Ottawa: Justice Canada.

Martyniuk, Waldemar, and José Noyons. 2006. *Executive summary of results of a survey on the use of the CEFR at national level in the Council of Europe Member States*. Strasbourg: Council of Europe.

Meyrowitz, Joshua. 2005. "The rise of glocality: new senses of place and identity in the global village." In *A Sense of Place: The Global and the Local in Mobile Communication*, edited by Kristof Nyiri, 21–30. Vienna: Passagen Verlag.

North, Brian, and Coreen Docherty. 2016. Forthcoming. "Validating a set of CEFR illustrative descriptors for mediation." *Research Notes* 63. Cambridge: Cambridge University Press.

North, Brian, and Günther Schneider. 1998. "Scaling descriptors for language proficiency scales." *Language Testing* 15(2): 217–262.

North, Brian, and Johanna Panthier. 2016. Forthcoming. "Updating the CEFR descriptors – The Context." *Research Notes* 63. Cambridge: Cambridge University Press.

North, Brian. 2000. *The Development of a Common Framework Scale of Language Proficiency*. New York: Peter Lang.

———. 2008. "Levels and Goals – Central Frameworks and Local Strategies." In *The Handbook of Educational Linguistics*, edited by Bernard Spolsky, 220–232. Malden MA and Oxford, UK: Blackwell.

———. 2014. "The CEFR in Practice." *English Profile Studies Series* 4. Cambridge: Cambridge University Press.

Pawlikowska-Smith, Grazyna. 2000. *Canadian Language Benchmarks 2000: English as a Second Langauge for Adults*. Ottawa: Centre for Canadian Language Benchmarks.

Piccardo, Enrica, Aline Germain-Rutherford and Richard Clement, eds. 2011. "Adopter ou adapter: le Cadre européen commun de référence est-il seulement européen?" *Synergies Europe* 6. Accessed February 27, 2016. http://gerflint.fr/Base/Europe6/Europe6.html.

———. 2014. *Du communicatif à l'actionnel: un cheminement de recherche*. Project "From Communicative to Action-Oriented: Illuminating the

Approaches," Ministry of Education Ontario. Accessed February 27, 2016. http://www.curriculum.org/storage/241/1410360061/TAGGED_DOCUMENT_%28CSC605_Research_Guide%3B_French%29_03.pdf

Ritzer, George, and Zach Ritzer. 2012. "Still enamoured of the glocal: a comment on 'From local to global, and back'." *Business History* 54(5): 798–804.

Rizvi, Fazal, and Bob Lingard. 2010. *Globalizing Education Policy*. London: Routledge.

Roudometof, Victor. 2015. "Theorizing glocalization: Three interpretations." *European Journal of Social Theory*: 1-18. DOI: 10.1177/1368431015605443.

Statistics Canada. 2012. *Linguistic Characteristics of Canadians. Language, 2011 Census of Population*. Ottawa: Industry Canada.

Treasury Board of Canada Secretariat. 2015. *Qualification Standards in Relation to Official Languages*. Accessed December 20, 2015. https://www.tbs-sct.gc.ca/gui/squntb-eng.asp.

Williams, Collin. 1998. "Introduction: Respecting the Citizens – Reflections on Language Policy in Canada and the United States." In *Language and Politics in the United States and Canada: Myths and Realities*, edited by Tom Ricento and Barbara Burnaby, 1–32. Mahwah, N.J.: Lawrence Erlbaum.

Notes

1. "Immigrant" is the preferred term in Canada, while "migrant" is commonly used in Europe. In this text, both terms are used in their respective contexts.
2. The term "Canadianity" refers to Canadian values and identity.
3. The term "allophone" refers to native speakers of languages other than French or English.
4. The descriptors for several aspects of mediation have recently been validated in a 2014–2016 project drawing on the methodology used in the Swiss project (North and Panthier 2016 forthcoming, North and Docherty 2016 forthcoming).
5. There are six levels in the CEFR versus twelve in the CLB/NCLC; four modes of language activity: reception, production, interaction, and mediation, each of which can be expressed orally or in writing in the CEFR, versus four language skills – oral and written comprehension, and oral and written production – in the CLB/NCLC.

CHAPTER 2

Design-Based Research Methodology for Establishing the Common Theoretical Framework and the CLB/NCLC Scales

Monique Bournot-Trites
University of British Columbia

1. Introduction

The *Canadian Language Benchmarks* (CLB) (CIC and CCLB 2012a) and the *Niveaux de competence linguistique canadiens* (NCLC) (CIC and CCLB 2012b) are language scales implemented by the Ministry of Immigration mainly for assessing the official language competency level of adult immigrants. However, these language scales are also used in teaching official languages and for other purposes related to language teaching and learning (see Introduction). In this chapter, I use the development of three documents – the common theoretical framework (Bournot-Trites et al. 2015), the CLB scale, and the NCLC scale – to illustrate how the Centre for Canadian Language Benchmarks (CCLB) develops guides and tools related to official-language learning and assessment based on research. I first review design-based research (Brown 1992, Collins 1992, Collins, Joseph, and Bielaczyc 2004), which was the method used to establish the theoretical framework and the benchmarks themselves. After acknowledging the origins of design-based research, I describe its characteristics, and then show how the theoretical framework and the benchmarks were developed and validated following this method. Finally, I conclude with the benefits of using this methodology in the field of second-language teaching, learning, and assessment.

2. Design-Based Research

Definition

Design-based research, or "Design Experiment" as it was called in its beginnings, is a relatively new methodology born out of the work of Ann Brown (1992) and Alan Collins (1992). When working in early-childhood classrooms, Brown found that the traditional experimental research was not entirely adequate. She noticed that collaboration with teachers was very important to inform her research; in fact, just as important as theories and published empirical research. Indeed, traditional empirical research starts with establishing hypotheses based on theories and previous empirical research related to the questions for which the researcher wants answers. Then experiments are conducted to test the stated hypotheses, and the data obtained are analysed. Results of the analyses give answers to the research questions, which in turn leads to refinement of the theories. Finally, the practitioners apply the new findings when they are disseminated; that is, if they find about them, which is not always the case.

Unlike traditional empirical research, design-based research involves practitioners right from the start of the investigation. According to the definition proposed by Wang and Hannafin (2005, 6), design-based research has "a systematic but flexible methodology aimed to improve educational practices through iterative analysis, design, development, and implementation, based on collaboration among researchers and practitioners in real-world settings, and leading to contextually sensitive design principles and theories."

Based on the literature, the same authors (Wang and Hannafin 2005, 7) list five important characteristics of design-based research:

(a) pragmatic;
(b) grounded;
(c) interactive, iterative, and flexible;
(d) integrative; and
(e) contextual.

First, design-based research is pragmatic, because the goal is to answer real-world questions by actually designing and creating products or interventions, as well as by adding to theories. As Cobb, Confrey, diSessa, Lehrer, and Shauble (2003, 10) wrote about design-based research in their conclusion, theories "do real work" in the field, as they bring important improvements in education. Problems or questions studied through design-based research are real problems found in education contexts.

Second, design-based research is said to be grounded in both theory and practice. It is "a commitment to theory construction and explanation while solving real-world problems" (Reeves, Herrington, and Oliver 2005, 103). Often, research questions come from needs in the field. Then, researchers choose a theory best suited to the question and find gaps in the related research literature. For example, if teachers wanted to provide support to readers who have difficulties in the primary years and if they wanted, at the same time, to give some leadership experience to their older students, they could discuss possible solutions with researchers. Then researchers would look at research done in peer tutoring and see which theoretical framework would be the best fit to the question, what research had already been done on the topic, and what the gaps were so they could propose interventions. Then they would work with the teachers to formulate research questions in order to solve the problem and at the same time advance reading theory. On one hand, the theoretical side of the process is important because without the theory such an endeavour would only result in the evaluation of the intervention or the program put in place and would not lead to theory development. On the other hand, it can be said that theory gets valued to the extent that it can be shown to improve practice, so it is important to have both researchers and practitioners working together before implementing a new product or intervention. Furthermore, design-based research is grounded in the natural context of the real world, where not all variables can be controlled for, as could be the case in the artificial setting of a laboratory. However, the results of design-based research are more directly and easily applicable to the real world than pure laboratory research.

Third, the design process in design-based research is interactive, iterative, and flexible. Collaboration between researchers and practitioners in a complementary fashion is essential so that the perspectives, knowledge, and expertise of each group can contribute to the benefit of the design. Therefore, there is a need for interaction between the two groups in a repetitive or iterative manner until the questions and interventions are agreed upon by all consensually.

Hence, design-based research is not imposed on practitioners by researchers and some flexibility is necessary to allow room for changes reflecting the perspectives of all members of the group to be represented in the final decisions.

Fourth, design-based research needs to be integrative, by drawing on different research methods that correspond to different needs. Mixed methods, including questionnaires, interviews, expert reviews, case studies, and comparative analysis using testing have the ability to answer a multitude of research questions. Anderson and Shattuck (2012), who reviewed the research methods used in design-based research, indicated: "DBR [design-based research] is largely agnostic when it comes to epistemological challenges to the choice of methodologies used and typically involves mixed methods using a variety of research tools and techniques" (17).

Finally, design-based research is contextual, that is "given the assumption that comparable performance is most likely in similar settings, contextually relevant design principles and knowledge are important for design-based researchers" (Wang and Hannafin 2005, 12). Consequently, careful notes have to be kept on the context in which the results were obtained, including the design process and the setting of the research. That way, other researchers or practitioners are able to examine the results in the light of their own context and needs.

Implementing design-based research

A list of steps are recommended (Jacobsen 2014, Reeves, Herrington, and Oliver 2005) when implementing a design-based research.

The first phase of the research project includes analysis and exploration. Initially, a meaningful problem, in particular a problem identified in the field by learners, educators, or other people, puts the research project in motion. Then researchers and practitioners meet and collaborate from the beginning to the end of the research project. For this to work, a well-founded theory related to the real-word problem must be chosen to guide the project.

In the second phase, the design and construction of the implementation takes place. A literature review and a needs analysis are conducted to find the gaps in empirical research published on the topic and to generate the research questions. Based on the findings from the research questions, an intervention or a product is designed, as well as a plan of evaluation.

The third and final phase is concerned with evaluation and reflection. The implementation is tried out in the context where the problem was identified. Then it is tested and refined continually in an iterative process until everyone is satisfied. At that point, the impact of the intervention is evaluated in a formative way, which may change the characteristics and details of the intervention during several cycles, as well as affecting the theories that explain the findings. Ultimately, the design-based research is reported in different ways, first in a series of interim reports and then in journal articles or books, as more adjustments are made over time for continual improvements.

Summary

Design-based research emerged as a way to address the lack of context in laboratory experiments and in response to a motivation to solve real-world problems, and represents a significant new way of doing research in educational contexts. Indeed, as Collins, Joseph and Bielaczyc (2004, 21) assert: "They [design-based projects] fill a niche in the array of experimental methods that is needed to improve educational practices." After a little more than twenty-five years, this new methodology has been shown to present some challenges (Dede 2004). For example, Brown (1992) herself has noted that very large amounts of data were collected within designed-based research, generating higher costs in terms of time and money. In fact, Brown notes that the researchers often lacked enough time to score all the data or store them. Another limitation of this methodology is that with the iterative nature of the research, it may also prove difficult to know when to stop collecting data and adjusting the final results. Moreover, O'Donnell (2004) indicates that, with continuous adjustments, generalization of the findings may be challenging because it is difficult to identify which factors are influencing success. However, these challenges can be overcome if the project participants agree to avoid the trap of collecting too much data, and to limit the number of changes and improvements. Furthermore, a detailed description of the context could improve generalizability by guiding those who want to apply the findings to another context. Many benefits can be derived from using design-based research. This new methodology has reduced the gap between theory and practice, as well as between researchers and practitioners. In addition, when practitioners are involved in the research, they are more willing to endorse new tools or approaches and to disseminate them among their colleagues. Additionally, as Barab and Squire (2004, 2) affirm, "Such design research offers several benefits: research results that consider the role of social context and have better potential for influencing educational practice, tangible products, and programs that can be adopted elsewhere; and research results that are validated through the consequences of their use, providing consequential evidence or validity (Messick, 1992)."[1]

Consequential evidence or validity is of great significance when creating a language framework as the basis for measuring the language competence level of immigrants. It was one more reason for using this methodology when developing the theoretical framework as well as the CLB and NCLC scales.

3. Development of the Common Theoretical Framework and the CLB/NCLC Scales

As will be shown in this section, the CCLB works with real-world questions and, in general, its actions are grounded in theory and practice. Indeed, for any new endeavour undertaken by the Centre, the design process is interactive, iterative, and flexible, and mixed methods are used to answer questions. Finally, in a country with two official languages and a diversity of settings due to the geographical extent, context has to be taken into account during any research process. For example, a geographical representation of practitioners from different parts of the country and from the two official-languages groups during the various consultation stages is essential. In the same way, in the case of the common theoretical framework and the CLB and NCLC scales, detailed reports show how those tools were developed and how the validation process was conducted.

In this section, I describe how the theoretical framework and the CLB and NCLC scales were developed following the design-based research principles, where researchers and practitioners worked together to improve the theoretical framework and the scales.

Right from the start, the development of the common theoretical framework and the CLB and NCLC has been interactive, iterative, and flexible. Indeed, "When CIC (Citizenship and Immigration Canada) introduced the CLB Working Document (*Canadian Language Benchmarks: English as a Second Language for Adults* called *Working Document*) in 1996, the department made a commitment to revisit the document regularly to maintain its integrity and relevance, to address gaps and to enhance its accessibility" (Bournot-Trites et al. 2015, 7).

Furthermore, revisions led by the CCLB were always dictated by real-world needs, following consultation with stakeholders. The Centre continuously works in partnership with various Canadian sectors involved in teaching the official languages to adult immigrants, from ministries at the federal level to provincial departments or ministries, colleges, school boards, and language-teaching associations (see Introduction). Indeed, in the first year following its creation, the CCLB was already seeking the input of its clients to guide future endeavours. Again in 2008, another massive consultation was conducted, leading to the revision of the *Canadian Language Benchmarks*: "More than 1,300 people, representing multiple stakeholder groups, participated in the process." (Bournot-Trites et al. 2015, 8). At the same time, key stakeholders of the French as a second language community met to discuss the findings of the consultation and to make recommendations for the French scales. Many recommendations were made with different levels of urgency (see Bournot-Trites et al. 2015, 8–9, for a list of recommendations for the CLB and for the NCLC).

Thus, in 2010, the CCLB produced two new working documents related to the French and English scales: the *Canadian Language Benchmarks, Working Document*, based on the *Canadian Language Benchmarks 2000: English as a Second Language for Adults* (Pawlikowska-Smith 2000) and the *Niveaux de competence linguistique canadiens, Document de travail* (Sarrazin 2010), which included an updated French theoretical framework. However, the theoretical framework for the English benchmarks, *Canadian Language Benchmarks 2000: Theoretical Framework* (Pawlikowska-Smith 2002), upon which the original French framework was based, had not been revised at this time. For historical reasons, the French and English documents had not evolved in a synchronous way and were not analogous – for more details on the history of the CLB and NCLC, see the introduction chapter of *Theoretical Framework for the CLB and NCLC* (Bournot-Trites et al. 2015).

In 2010, the CCLB was set to answer the needs of the stakeholders about the English and the French scales. In order to be acceptable and recognized, the CLB and the NCLC had to undergo a validation study. The details of the validation process reported in this chapter have been described in unpublished reports (Bournot-Trites and Barbour 2012, Elson 2012a, 2012b).

Before beginning the validation study, the CCLB had asked a pan-Canadian team of experts in second-language learning and assessment to propose a detailed process in order to give direction to the validation study. It was then decided to create a common theoretical framework as a foundation for both the English and French scales, as well as a process to establish the construct validity and content validity of the CLB and NCLC. The following sections offer a description of the three phases of the validation study, showing how this process followed the main principles of design-based research. Figure 2.1 represents the validation process for Phases I and II.

Phase I: A common theoretical framework grounded in theory

During Phase I of the validation study, the primary objective was to establish the theory underpinning the CLB and NCLC, and to develop a common theoretical framework (CTF) for the CLB and NCLC working documents that were revised in 2010 (based on the previous French and English documents). The secondary objective was to verify how well the new common theoretical framework corresponded to the theories on which it was based. Both the joint project leads, as well as contributing researchers, reviewed, in detail, the CLB and the NCLC – that is the *Canadian Language Benchmarks 2000: Theoretical Framework* (Pawlikowska-Smith 2002) and the *Niveaux de competence linguistique canadiens, Document de travail* (Sarrazin 2010) – to identify the similarities and differences between them. After a careful comparison and synthesis of the theoretical concepts found in the two documents, a list of the core common concepts was established.

When writing the first draft of the common theoretical framework (CTF), the theories and research cited in each source document, as well as field studies in English as a second language (ESL) and French as a second language (FSL), were considered in order to improve the content of the original documents. Additionally, this first draft was validated by experts to make sure that the new theoretical framework faithfully represented the original documents and the theoretical concepts underlying them. Four experts were selected to undertake this validation, according to following criteria: they had to be specialists in language assessment, applied linguistics, or curriculum design; hold a Ph.D.; have done research in language assessment or applied linguistics; and have a basic knowledge of and experience with the CLB or the NCLC. Those experts had to answer

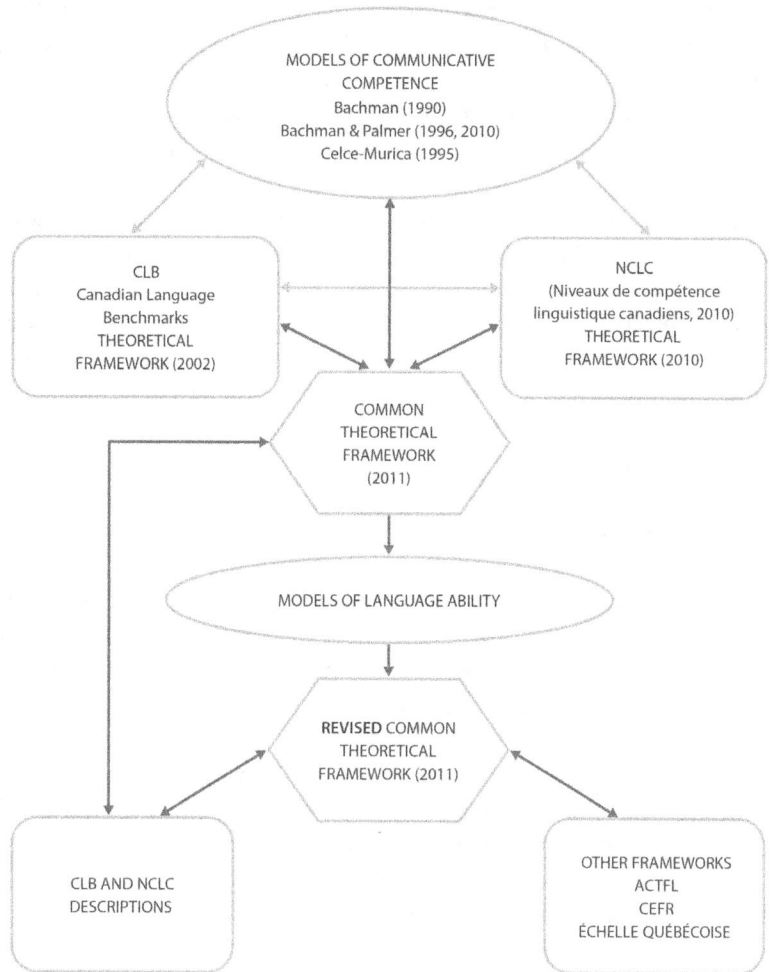

Figure 2.1: Diagram representing Phases I and II of the validation process of the CLB and NCLC
(Double arrows indicate a comparison. Dark arrows indicate verification done by independent experts.)
Source: Bournot-Trites, M. and R. Barbour. (2012) "Unpublished Report on Phases I and II of the Validation of the Canadian Language Benchmarks and Niveaux de Compétence Linguistique Canadiens." (reproduced with permission of the authors and CCLB)

a detailed questionnaire asking them to compare the first draft of the *Common Theoretical Framework* with the two source documents and with the theories on which they were based: the models of Bachman (1990), Bachman and Palmer (1996), and Celce-Murcia, Dörnyei, and Thurrell (1995), and on the 2010 updated model of Bachman and Palmer. Considering all these theories created difficulties, because the different models of Bachman (1990), Bachman and Palmer (1996, 2010), and Celce-Murcia et al. (1995), as well as the CLB and NCLC frameworks, had used different terms to discuss the same concepts. Therefore, to prevent confusion, the lead researchers created a concordance table (Bournot-Trites et al. 2015, 19 and Appendix A) to show the correspondence between labels and concepts. This essential step of the validation study shows that the work of the CCLB is grounded in theory, as described earlier in reference to design-based research.

From the results of the questionnaire answered by the experts, it was found that both theoretical frameworks were in step with the communicative approach (Germain 1991, Littlewood 1981) and with the functional approach (Halliday and Kirkwood 1974) to language use, and both were based on the three models: Bachman (1990), Bachman and Palmer (1996), and Celce-Murcia et al. (1995). Importantly, the model proposed by Celce-Murcia et al. was the primary focal point of both theoretical frameworks. As a next step, the project leads and the contributing researchers, along with CCLB staff, identified the strongest contributions from each theoretical framework and used the results to develop general guidelines for teaching and assessment that would be applicable to ESL and FSL. In addition, over the course of the validation activities, the expert panel determined that the updated Bachman and Palmer (2010) model, which was very similar to the 1996 one, should be given more importance than the Celce-Murcia et al. model, because it was more encompassing. Indeed, it was applicable to all instances of language use rather than only oral communication, as is the case in the Celce-Murcia et al. model, and was generally used in the broader fields of applied linguistics, second-language acquisition, and language testing, rather than only by ESL curriculum developers and practitioners (see table 3, p. 20, in Bournot-Trites et al. 2015 for a comparison of Bachman and Palmer 1996 and 2010 and Celce-Murcia et al. 1995). However, the Celce-Murcia et al. model was retained in an appendix, because it was an adaptation of the Bachman and Palmer model, and because it provided helpful concrete and detailed strategies to language teachers for use in the classroom.

In summary, Phase I answered a real-world problem as a result of a national consultation, then it made sure that the common theoretical framework reflected the two original frameworks while being grounded in the best and most up-to-date language development and assessment theories, as well as in language-teaching research.

Phase II: Content validity of the scales and concurrent validity of the common theoretical framework

As indicated above in the list of steps recommended in design-based research for projects (Jacobsen 2014, Reeves, Herrington, and Oliver 2005), Phase II was concerned with the construction and design of the implementation: the CLB and NCLC scales. In this case, a working version of the CLB and NCLC had already been created and used; therefore, the first part of this second phase had to do with verifying whether the CLB and NCLC corresponded to the common theoretical framework and revising them or the common theoretical framework if needed. Another part of the second phase was involved in establishing congruence between the CLB and NCLC common theoretical framework and other widely accepted frameworks.

Accordingly, the next step was to compare the descriptors contained in the CLB and NCLC scales and the new common theoretical framework. To do this, six independent experts were selected according to the same criteria as in the previous phase. However, to make sure there was consistency in the process, some experts had to work on both the CLB and the NCLC. Therefore, the six experts were selected from both ESL and FSL fields, with four of them being bilingual. This group of experts was made up of researchers and practitioners working together: researchers, curriculum designers, and language co-ordinators.

To carry out this correspondence-analysis task, the experts were provided with an Excel file for each skill – listening, reading, writing, speaking – in which each line of the first two columns was a component or subcomponent of communicative competence as described in the draft common theoretical framework according to Bachman and Palmer (2010) and Celce-Murcia et al. (1995), as well as *La Nouvelle Grammaire* (Chartrand et al. 1999, Pinsonneault and Boivin 2008, Riegel, Pellat, and Rioul 2009), a pedagogical approach to teaching grammar that was included in the NCLC framework. These first two columns were followed by twelve columns corresponding to the twelve benchmarks of each scale. The task of the experts was to match each descriptor with a corresponding component or subcomponent. In the case of a descriptor for which no corresponding component or subcomponent could be found, the descriptor had to be highlighted in the CLB or NCLC working document. Two experts were working on each stage (beginner, intermediate, and advanced scales), but they were asked to work individually at first and then together. They were each assigned a block of four benchmarks for each skill for the CLB and six benchmarks for each skill for the NCLC. In summary, their work was to find which elements of the theoretical framework were found in each benchmark and which descriptors did not correspond to any element of the theoretical framework. After their individual work, they attended a four-day meeting (two days for descriptors in English and two days for descriptors in French) where they compared their results with their partners and reached a consensus wherever there was disagreement. First, the two experts who had worked on the same descriptor levels compared their results to verify if they had the same results, then the entire panel discussed any point of disagreement. In addition, the panel discussed the broader congruence between the theoretical framework and the CLB and NCLC.

As a result of this analysis, several recommendations for revision to the descriptors were made. A detailed list of the recommendations can be found in the validation reports (Bournot-Trites and Barbour 2012, Elson 2012a, 2012b). Mainly it was suggested that, during the revision of the scales and before field testing, gaps found during the validation process be filled where it was developmentally appropriate. For example, some language functions might not be appropriate for beginners and therefore should not be included in the lowest benchmarks levels.

In general, it was noted that the CLB were congruent with the common theoretical framework; however, it was suggested that more elements of grammatical knowledge be included (including vocabulary, syntax, and morphology/graphology), as well as elements of the strategic competence in individual CLB levels when these elements had a clear logical link with the descriptors at a particular level. The panel also found that pronunciation and grammar elements were stated according to a deficit model – in terms of how they hampered communication – and it was recommended that they be stated in a positive manner, as what the learner could do, instead.

On the other hand, the NCLC were generally found to be **not** congruent with the theories on which they were supposedly based. All the elements of the common theoretical framework could be found in the NCLC descriptors, but their sequencing was not always logical. The validation report (Bournot-Trites and Barbour 2012, 12) stated: "The panel recommended a significant revision of the indicators used to show progression by, a), providing more information about performance within the indicators and, b), revising the presentation and progression of indicators and 'Profil de l'apprenant' in a way which would allow users to better track the progression of language ability through the levels."

Furthermore, no elements of *La Nouvelle Grammaire* (Chartrand et al. 1999) were found in the descriptors of the NCLC; therefore, this theoretical aspect was taken out of the common theoretical framework and only retained in an appendix related to pedagogy.

The panel also provided feedback on the assessment and pedagogy sections of the common theoretical framework. Their recommendations were mainly editorial in nature. One major recommendation was to include self-assessment and peer assessment as ways to evaluate strategic competence and cognitive strategies that are difficult to observe directly from the production of the learners.

After the examination of the congruence between the common theoretical framework and the CLB and the NCLC, and once the recommendations for revisions in all the documents were submitted, the CTF was examined in terms of concurrent validity with the Common European Framework of Reference (CEFR) (Council of Europe 2001), the *American Council on the Teaching of Foreign Language Proficiency Guidelines* (ACTFL Guidelines) (American Council for the Teaching of Foreign Language 1982, American Council on the Teaching of Foreign Languages 1999), and *L'Échelle québécoise des niveaux de compétences en langue seconde pour les immigrants adultes* (EQ) (Gouvernement du Québec 2011). The CEFR and the ACTFL Guidelines were chosen because they are well recognized and have a long history of development, and the EQ was chosen because it was a Quebecois reference.

For this theoretical concurrent validity process, a standardized questionnaire, including twenty-four questions, was sent to four experts who had in-depth knowledge of the common theoretical framework as well as the other frameworks. The questionnaire was sent in French to the experts analysing the *Échelle Québécoise*. Thus, the revised common theoretical framework was validated against each of the three other frameworks by two independent academics with expertise in their respective frameworks. The main themes guiding the questions were: theoretical model, number of skills, concept of a benchmark, task as a basic element, functional approach, knowledge types (textual, grammatical, cultural, sociolinguistic), strategic competence, pedagogy, and assessment.

From this analysis, the CEFR was found to have many similarities with the Common Theoretical Framework. There were some differences in categorization of elements between the two frameworks. In addition, the CEFR showed its greater maturity through more expansion of basic elements and in assessment development. One major difference between the two frameworks was the number of skills. The CLB and NCLC have four skills (writing, reading, listening, and speaking), whereas the CEFR has four modes (reception, interaction, production, and mediation), each split into spoken and written, which results in eight skills. The validity report states: "From this analysis by our experts, it became clear that the Common Theoretical Framework and the CEFR had many similarities. There are no fundamental differences between them. Where there are differences, they are mainly expansions of basic elements in the CEFR, probably due to the maturity of, and the multi-national resources behind, the framework" (Bournot-Trites and Barbour 2012, 18).

In contrast, the new CTF was found to have a low concurrent validity with the ACTFL Guidelines for two reasons: because of a discrepancy between the goals of the two frameworks, and because the ACTFL Guidelines are not based on a theoretical framework but on the examiners' experience. Indeed, their construct validity has been criticized by researchers in the field of language testing (Bachman and Savignon 1986, Fulcher 1996, Liskin-Gasparro 2003). Liskin-Gasparro (2003) wrote in her review of the ACTFL Guidelines, and particularly the Oral Proficiency Interview (OPI):

> A review of the research and critiques on the ACTFL Guidelines and the OPI (see Freed, 1988; Liskin-Gasparro, 2000) leads to the conclusion that proficiency as described in the ACTFL Guidelines is far less absolute and broad based than the early proponents had claimed. Its empirical basis is shaky, and its

claim to be conversational does not hold up. It is clear that oral proficiency ratings predict far less about an individual's future performance in a range of communicative situations than promoters of the OPI would like them to. (488)

As for the EQ, it was difficult to compare it to the new common theoretical framework because it was not a theoretical framework as such but, as its name indicates, only a scale. However, although the EQ terminology is adapted to the Quebecois context, it is inspired by the NCLC as well as the CEFR (Gouvernement du Québec 2011) and is based on a communicative approach. The summary of the validation report (Bournot-Trites and Barbour 2012, 23) indicates that "the independent experts did not identify any direct contradiction between the EQ and the CTF."

In summary, this second phase established the theoretical content and concurrent validity of the CLB and NCLC. This was done by linking theory and practice, as well as researchers and practitioners, as shown in the description of Phase II of the validation study. As a result, revisions were made to the CLB and the NCLC and to the common theoretical framework. This phase was followed by a study of the content validity of the descriptors in a repeated cycle of revisions, trials, and reflection.

Phase III of the validation process: Field validation

Phase III, determining the validity and reliability of the revised CLB and NCLC scales, was a very important step of the process, where practitioners were brought back into the project again. After establishing a common theoretical framework based on the most recognized theories related to language teaching and assessment, and verifying the congruence of the common theoretical framework with the CLB and NCLC descriptors and other recognized language frameworks, the goal of Phase III was to "establish whether practitioners who have experience with and understanding of the benchmarks, see the revised CLB and NCLC as valid and accurate descriptors of authentic language performance" (Elson 2012b, 1, 2012a, 1). This third phase aimed also at establishing reliability of the CLB and NCLC, that is, finding out if various people would interpret the revised benchmarks in the same way. For the purpose of this chapter, since the same method was used for both CLB and NCLC, only the process with CLB is reported here.

At the beginning of Phase III, a team of content developers created authentic tasks and scenarios – 89 listening tasks, 25 speaking tasks, 109 reading tasks, and 24 writing tasks – reflecting benchmarks for each skill. It is important to note that the produced exemplars were authentic and that the scenarios corresponded to several benchmarks, rather than to one particular benchmark.

Then the field validation was done in two steps by two groups. First, a group of experts reviewed the descriptors and exemplars for each skill at each level, and second, a larger group of practitioners worked on the validation and reliability *per se* of the CLB. This method ensured that the perspective of experts, as well as that of the practitioners, was taken into account and that they were in agreement.

In the first step, a panel of six experts was selected after a call for expression of interest was distributed as widely as possible. The selection criteria were very precise and included knowledge of the CLB, experience in teaching applied linguistics or second-language pedagogy, training in ESL teaching, and scholarly activity (including conference presentations and publications), as well as geographic representation. This ensured that experts really were experts in the appropriate areas.

Once the experts were chosen, the validation task was sent to them, along with the exemplars. Their responsibility was to assign "what they saw as the lowest appropriate CLB level necessary, to effectively carry out those tasks or to describe the language samples provided" (Elson 2012a, 2). A high correlation between the experts would indicate a high reliability. "A high degree of correlation among raters in the benchmark levels assigned to the exemplars and tasks also validates the benchmark descriptors for each task" (6). Besides attributing a benchmark to each exemplar, the experts were given a second task. They had to judge the authenticity and representativeness of each descriptor compared to language use, via a four-point Likert scale: 1-Not Representative; 2-Representative with substantial revision; 3-Representative with minor revisions; 4-Representative. This second task would help to establish the validity of the descriptors.

Based on the six responses of the experts, the validation project lead determined the final benchmark level for each exemplar. Calculated inter-rater reliability coefficients ranged from .83 to .89, indicating strong reliability. Validity of the descriptors was equally high, as shown by the content validity index (CVI), "No combined CVI ratings for 3 and 4 fell below 0.83. This result supports confidence in the content validity of the revised CLB" (Elson 2012a, 12).

Importantly, the form given to the experts allowed for additional commentary by the raters. One key comment received was about the difficulty of distinguishing some benchmark levels from adjacent ones. As a result, those benchmarks were revised to add more differentiation points between successive descriptors. Another type of comment suggested changing the level of some descriptors, especially in stage 2. This important feedback afforded more refinement of the benchmarks and increased their validity. The author of the report (Elson 2012a, 12) indicated: "Taken overall, the calculations of Interrater Reliability (IRR), the Content Validity Index (CVI), and the expert rater comments all support the conclusion that the revised CLB have strong content validity and a high level of reliability. Six experts, acting independently, have been able to essentially agree on the accuracy of the revised benchmark descriptors."

Following the experts' validation work, field practitioners were called on for a "validity and reliability exercise" to further establish "the degree to which the content of the revised benchmarks is authentic, relevant and representative of the larger language framework and the constructs from which they are sampled" (Elson 2012a, 12). Practitioners have real-world experience and knowledge of the benchmarks from a user point of view, which is very important in assessing the validity and reliability of a measuring instrument such as the CLB or the NCLC.

Out of 110 practitioners contacted, sixty-one contributed to the validity and reliability tasks. They represented all benchmarks levels, but more often the lowest stages of the benchmarks, and all regions of Canada, but especially Ontario and British Columbia, where there are more ESL programs. Criteria for selecting practitioners included extensive experience teaching a second language to adults in Canada, access to a classroom, and extensive familiarity with the benchmarks.

The practitioners were provided with a response form for each of the four skills, and a chart including all the scenarios and exemplars/tasks reviewed by the expert with the benchmark level assigned to each after the work of the panel of experts, as well as the recordings, videos, and print materials related to the tasks. Practitioners had to indicate, using a four-point Likert scale, if each of the descriptors was authentic and representative of the target language use – 4 being the most representative and 1 the least. Then they had to indicate if the level agreed upon by the expert panel for each task was just right, too high, or too low, and provide an alternative level if applicable. Finally, practitioners were invited to give comments on the two parts, of their task, validity and reliability.

The results indicated that 80 percent or more of the responses about the authenticity and representativeness of the descriptors were within the 3 and 4 ratings, except for benchmark 6 (across all four skills). In summary, the report declared that, "these figures indicate that across a wide range of practitioners, the results for Part 1 show strong support for the content validity of the revised benchmarks" (Elson 2012a, 18). These ratings, coupled with the comments, provided opportunities to make the descriptors even more efficient and valid.

The second part of the exercise provided more evidence of the validity of the levels assigned to the tasks and the reliability of the benchmarks themselves, "since a high level of agreement on ratings for particular tasks indicates that the benchmarks are clear and accurate in their description, and can be used and applied repeatedly in a reliable and consistent way across programs and field practitioners" (Elson 2012a, 19). Results showed a high percentage of practitioners indicating that the benchmark level assigned to each task was just right: 79 percent for the listening tasks, 76 percent for the speaking tasks, 80 percent for the reading tasks, and 82 percent for the writing tasks, respectively. When three alternative ratings were given for a task, it was recommended that the task be examined to see if an alternative benchmark designation was appropriate. Furthermore, all comments, such as those explaining why an alternative benchmark designation was suggested, or other comments given by practitioners, were analysed and consideration was given to making more changes to the benchmarks or to improving training of the practitioners. Many of the comments were positive, emphasising the improvement made to the benchmarks. In summary, the report (Elson 2012a, 25) states that, "In Part 2, the field practitioners indicated overall agreement with the benchmark levels assigned by the experts to the tasks and exemplars in each skill category. This tells us that for most of the respondents, the tasks are seen as valid in that they accurately reflect the benchmark levels assigned to them."

In this Phase III of the validation, one can clearly see an iterative work of validation calling upon expert theoreticians as well as practitioners to establish the degree of validity and reliability of the scales. Furthermore, the detailed reports of Phases I, II, and III give the context and various methods with which this validation has been established, and describe the care with which the scales were adjusted and refined, taking into account a wide array of users and researchers. Undeniably, this illustration of design-based research at work is very different from the traditional experimental method that was found inadequate by Brown (1992). It stems from real-world problems, it is as much grounded in theory as it is in the experience of practitioners, it creates bridges between the two groups and takes into account their different perspectives to produce more adequate and valid results, and it engages practitioners in new endeavours and ensures that the findings of research will be applied in the field. In sum, it is more suitable for educational research than more traditional research methodologies.

4. Conclusion

Design-based research is a relatively new methodology that shows great potential in being more appropriate in education than traditional research methods. The field of language teaching and assessment is strongly rooted in theories of language and language acquisition. However, language is used in the real world and usage evolves. Therefore, research in language assessment can neither be cut from theories nor from practice. Research questions and problems related to language assessment can be born from practice as much as from theories. The example of the revision of the CLB and the NCLC theoretical framework and scales has shown that it was problem-driven and that practitioners initiated the revisions by expressing a need to improve the existing scales. In turn, researchers used theories to guide the reformulation of the theoretical framework and collaborated with experts and practitioners to validate the revised documents and fine-tune them. They used a variety of methods, including a survey, questionnaires, open-ended questions, expert reviews, statistical analyses, and consensus building, to arrive at a product that is more satisfactory for all its users. In this way, researchers generated a new theoretical framework and two scales, the CLB and the NCLC, which were tried out in authentic contexts. Practitioners in collaboration with experts were able to demonstrate consequential validity (Messick 1989) through their analysis and feedback. Such a design-based research methodology created a bridge between theory and practice and between researchers and practitioners, improving practice and theory in tandem.

Taken together, the different phases of the revision of the CLB and the NCLC and the validation studies demonstrate that the CLB and the NCLC have a strong content validity and reliability. After the refinement of the benchmarks following those studies, researchers and practitioners can use them with confidence, knowing that they rest on a strong theoretical basis and are empirically sound. This would not be possible if they had been developed only by researchers based on theories or only by practitioners based on experience.

The strength of the CLB and the NCLC comes from the design-based research methodology used to improve them. Two distinctive features of this method are crucial in any assessment endeavour: consideration of a diversity of perspectives and involvement of a variety of stakeholders. First, the theoretical frameworks as well as the scales have been examined, analysed, and critiqued by different stakeholders offering a variety of perspectives, knowledge, experience, and expertise. This approach improved the Common Theoretical Framework (CTF) and the scales, and in turn made them more valid. As Brandon (1998) has shown, evaluators who use the expertise of all suitable stakeholders through careful methods of data collection ensure that they increase evaluation validity. Second, in general, people value more highly the products they participate in creating. In this case, because stakeholders were involved in the co-creation and validation of the CTF and the scales, they and the people they represent, such as researchers, curriculum developers, and language co-ordinators, will value them more. Involving a variety of stakeholders in this process will bring change in language assessment in Canada by creating a higher level of engagement of users. Involvement through representatives increases ownership and therefore the feeling of control, which in turn brings commitment. Because of this partnership, the likelihood of the scales being acceptable and therefore accepted by users in the field is amplified, and the CLB and NCLC stand to become models for other language descriptors.

References

American Council on the Teaching of Foreign Languages. 1982. *Provisional Proficiency Guidelines*. New York: Hasting on Hudson.

———. 1999. *ACTFL Proficiency Guidelines for Speaking (Revised)*. Accessed May 30, 2016. http://www.actfl.org/files/public/Guidelinesspeak.pdf.

Anderson, Terry, and Julie Shattuck. 2012. "Design-Based Research: A Decade of Progress in Education Research?" *Educational Researcher* 41(1): 16–25.

Bachman, Lyle F. 1990. *Fundamental Considerations in Language Testing*. Oxford: Oxford University Press.

Bachman, Lyle F., and Adrian Palmer. 1996. *Language Testing in Practice: Designing and Developing Useful Language Tests*. New York: Oxford University Press.

———. 2010. *Language Assessment Practice: Developing Language Assessments and Justifying Their Use in the Real World*. New York: Oxford University Press.

Bachman, Lyle F., and Sandra J. Savignon. 1986. "The Evaluation of Communicative Language Proficiency: A Critique of the ACTFL Oral Interview." *Modern Language Journal* 70(4): 380–390.

Barab, Sasha, and Kurt Squire. 2004. "Introduction: Design-Based Research: Putting a Stake in the Ground." *The Journal of the Learning Sciences* 13(1): 1–14.

Bournot-Trites, Monique, Ross Barbour, Monika Jezak, Gail Stewart, and Daphné Blouin Carbonneau. 2015. *Theoretical Framework for the CLB and NCLC*. Ottawa: Citizenship and Immigration Canada.

Bournot-Trites, Monique, and Ross Barbour. 2012. Unpublished Report on Phases I and II of the Validation of the Canadian Language Benchmarks and Niveaux de Compétence Linguistique Canadiens. Ottawa: Centre for Canadian Language Benchmarks.

Brandon, Paul R. 1998. "Stakeholder participation for the purpose of helping ensure evaluation validity: Bridging the gap between collaborative and non-collaborative evaluations." *American Journal of Evaluation* 19(3): 325-337.

Brown, Ann L. 1992. "Design Experiments: Theoretical and Methodological Challenges in Creating Complex Interventions in Classroom Settings." *The Journal of the Learning Sciences* 2(2): 141–178.

Celce-Murcia, Marianne, Zoltan Dörnyei, and Sarah Thurrell. 1995. "Communicative Competence: A Pedagogically Motivated Model with Content Specifications." *Issues in Applied Linguistics* 6(2): 5–35.

Chartrand, Suzanne-G., Denis Aubin, Raymond Blain and Claude Simard. 1999. *Grammaire Pédagogique du Français d'aujourd'hui*. Boucherville: Graficor-La Chenelière.

Citizenship and Immigration Canada. 1996. *Canadian Language Benchmarks: English as a Second Language for Adults. English as a second language for literacy learners (working document)*. Ottawa: Minister of Supply and Services Canada.

Citizenship and Immigration Canada, and Centre for Canadian Language Benchmarks. 2012a. *Canadian Language Benchmarks: English as a Second Language for Adults*. Ottawa: Citizenship and Immigration Canada.

———. 2012b. *Niveaux de compétence linguistique canadiens : français langue seconde pour adultes*. Ottawa: Citizenship and Immigration Canada.

Cobb, Paul, Jere Confrey, Andrea diSessa, Richard Lehrer, and Leona Schauble. 2003. "Design Experiments in Educational Research." *Educational Researcher* 32(1): 9–13.

Collins, Allan. 1992. "Toward a Design Science of Education." In *New Directions in Educational Technology*, edited by Eileen Scanlon, and Tim O'Shea, 15–22. Berlin: Springer Verlag.

Collins, Allan, Diana Joseph, and Katerine Bielaczyc. 2004. "Design Research: Theoretical and Methodological Issues." *The Journal of the Learning Sciences* 13(1): 15–42.

Conseil de l'Europe. 2001. *Cadre Européen Commun de Référence pour les Langues: Apprendre, Enseigner, Évaluer*. Paris: Didier.

Dede, Chris. 2004. "If Design-Based Research Is the Answer, What Is the Question? A Commentary on Collins, Joseph, and Bielaczyc; Disessa and Cobb; and Fishman, Marx, Blumenthal, Krajcik, and Soloway in the Jls Special Issue on Design-Based Research." *Journal of the Learning Sciences* 13(1): 105–114. doi: 10.1207/s15327809jls1301_5.

Elson, Nicholas. 2012a. Unpublished Final Report on the Benchmarking of the Revised Canadian Language Benchmarks (CLB) by the Expert Panel and Field Practitioners. Ottawa: Centre for Canadian Language Benchmarks.

———. 2012b. Unpublished Final Report on the Benchmarking of the Revised Niveaux De Compétences Linguistique Canadiens (NCLC) by the Expert Panel and Field Practitioners. Ottawa: Centre for Canadian Language Benchmarks.

Fulcher, Glenn. 1996. "Invalidating Validity Claims for the ACTFL Oral Rating Scale." *System* 24(2): 163–172.

Germain, Claude, ed. 1991. *Le Point sur l'approche communicative en didactique des langues*. Montreal: CEC.

Government of Quebec. 2011. *L'échelle Québecoise des Niveaux de Compétence en Français pour les Personnes Immigrantes Adultes*. Montréal: MICC-MELS.

Halliday, Michael, and Alexander Kirkwood. 1974. La Base Fonctionnelle du Langage. *Langages* 34:53–73.

Jacobsen, Michele. 2014. "Design-Based Research." *Education Canada* 54(5): 22–24.

Liskin-Gasparro, Judith E. 2003. "The ACTFL Proficiency Guidelines and the Oral Proficiency Interview: A Brief History and Analysis of Their Survival." *Foreign Language Annals* 36(4): 483–490. doi: 10.1111/j.1944-9720.2003.tb02137.x.

Littlewood, William. 1981. *Communicative Language Teaching: An Introduction*. Cambridge, New York: Cambridge University Press.

Messick, Samuel. 1989. "Validity." In *Educational Measurement*. 3rd edition. Edited by Robert L. Linn, 13–103. London: Collier Macmillan Publishers.

O'Donnell, Angela M. 2004. "A Commentary on Design Research." *Educational Psychologist* 39(4): 255–260. doi: 10.1207/s15326985ep3904_7.

Pawlikowska-Smith, Grazyna. 2000. *Canadian Language Benchmarks 2000: English as a Second Langauge for Adults*. Ottawa: Centre for Canadian Language Benchmarks.

———. 2002. *Canadian Language Benchmarks 2000: Theoretical Framework*. Ottawa: Centre for Canadian Language Benchmarks.

Pinsonneault, Reine, and Marie-Claude Boivin. 2008. *La Grammaire Moderne: Description et Éléments pour sa Didactique*. Montreal: Beauchemin/Chenelière Éducation.

Reeves, Thomas C., Jan Herrington and Ron Oliver. 2005. "Design Research: A Socially Responsible Approach to Instructional Technology Research in Higher Education." *Journal of Computing in Higher Education* 16(2): 96–115.

Riegel, Martin, Jean-Christophe Pellat, and René Rioul 2009. *Grammaire Méthodique du Français*. Paris: PUF.

Sarrazin, George. 2010. *Niveaux de Compétence Linguistiques Canadiens: Français Langue Seconde Pour Adultes (Document De Travail)*. Ottawa: Centre des niveaux de compétence linguistique canadiens.

Wang, Feng, and Michael J. Hannafin. 2005. "Design-Based Research and Technology-Enhanced Learning Environments." *Educational Technology Research and Development* 53(4): 5–23. doi: 10.1007/BF02504682.

Note

1   Messick originated the expression "consequential evidence or validity."

CHAPTER 3

Teaching and Assessment with the CLB: Teacher Experiences and Perspectives

Eve Haque and Antonella Valeo
York University

The importance of classroom-based official-language instruction for newcomers cannot be overstated. Almost half of the immigrants surveyed as part of the Longitudinal Survey of Immigrants to Canada (Chui 2003) participated in adult immigrant English-language training and, of this group, 85 percent found English-language training classes to be useful or very useful (Smit and Turcot 2010). Thus, the development of the *Canadian Language Benchmarks* (CLB) is arguably one of the most significant endeavours to come out of the publicly funded arena of English as a second language in Canada. As such, the importance of the CLB for programming and instruction in these classes across Canada cannot be underestimated. Although described as a "foundation of shared philosophical and theoretical views on language ability that informs language instruction and assessment" (CIC and CCLB 2012, v), it is how the CLB ultimately inform language instruction in the classroom that is the focus of this chapter. The CLB are clearly labelled as a set of descriptive statements about communicative competencies and levels on a continuum of language ability, and a *standard* and *reference framework* for planning curriculum for teaching and learning. As well, it is clearly laid out what the CLB are **not**; that is, not a curriculum, instructional method, or assessment, nor are they a description of the discrete elements of knowledge and skills underlying communicative competence, such as cultural conventions, vocabulary, micro-functions, or grammatical structures (CIC and CCLB 2012, v).

Although it has been made clear that the CLB are not a curriculum, there is evidence that instructors continue to draw directly on the CLB to frame and organize their teaching practice in ways that they might do from a curriculum. Teachers in adult language training classrooms have to consider a number of issues when they are organizing their teaching. They have to incorporate learner needs as well as institutional requirements, constraints, and curricular mandates into their planning (Wette 2009). These issues are complicated even further across Canada, as instructors must balance their own autonomy with the need to inform their curricular planning with the institutionally organized and mandated CLB framework. This raises interesting questions about how teachers understand the place of the CLB in developing their classroom practice and how this understanding is mediated through their training, experience, and teaching contexts. In this chapter, we examine some particular facets of the CLB standards to understand how teaching and assessment is represented with regards to classroom practice, and we draw on research – including interviews with teachers – to explore these questions.

In 2010, the final report of the national consultation on the CLB 2000 was published (Smit and Turcot 2010). The consultation process included forums, interviews, and surveys to collect feedback from multiple stakeholders across the country, including instructors, learners, administrators, academics, and others who were users or in other ways had an impact on the CLB. The consultation asked stakeholders to identify the top three strengths of the document and responses were categorized according to different features of the document, including strengths related to the framework and its constructs, those aspects of the document that supported teaching and curriculum, the value of the CLB as a national standard, and the role of the CLB in assessment. Analysis of practitioner responses showed that 50 percent of focus-group participants cited aspects relevant to the value of the framework and its constructs, 19 percent described strengths relevant to CLB as a national standard, nearly 16 percent identified the role of the CLB in assessment, and almost 12 percent cited the CLB as a support for teaching and curriculum. When asked to rate aspects of the CLB according to value, over 80 percent of practitioners gave three specific aspects of the CLB the highest ratings: "a national framework for understanding and measuring language proficiency";

"a common language for stakeholders across the country"; and "comprehensive – covers all four aspects of language proficiency" (Smit and Turcot 2010, 10). Clearly the documents spoke to gaps for practitioners who saw the relevance of the CLB as a national standard, a tool for assessment, and support for teaching and curriculum, and drew on these views when implementing the CLB in their practice. In the first part of the chapter, we look at three specific features of the CLB: the notion of a continuum of development, the role of task (a framework for assessment), and how these features relate to the role of assessment as teachers apply the CLB to classroom contexts. In the second part of the chapter, we draw on teachers' own thoughts about how the CLB informs their classroom practice as a framework for instruction.

1. A Framework for Assessment

The CLB have been used as a framework for assessment both inside and outside the classroom. Outside the classroom, two primary standardized tests have been developed, the long-standing *Canadian Language Benchmarks Assessment* (CLBA), used in the original Language Instruction for Newcomers to Canada (LINC) program for placement of learners, and the streamlined version, the *Canadian Language Benchmarks Placement Test* (CLBPT), developed for wider use in ESL programs. In the classroom, the CLB are used in formative and summative ways. The *CLB 5-10 Exit Assessment Tasks* were developed to guide formative assessment intended to help teachers move learners across courses within a program or in some cases exit the program. The summative assessment tool, *Summative Assessment Manual for CLB Stage 1* (CLB 1-4), helps instructors plan instruction and support learners, while learners are able to use this information to direct their own learning as well. The diversity in this array of documents represents an attempt to respond to the needs of practitioners as they implement the CLB into their programs to support language assessment.

Another support document that attempted to address the challenges of CLB-based assessment is *Integrating CLB Assessment into your ESL Classroom* (Holmes 2005). This document draws on the distinction between assessment *of* learning and assessment *for* learning, and acknowledges the "tensions" inherent for teachers in classroom-based assessment. This highlights the challenge of playing a supportive role for learners while, at the same time, participating in summative decision making that may carry a high-stakes impact on program and funding access, and employment opportunities. The document also draws attention to the complexity of language in that a document such as the CLB may not fully capture the range of an individual's abilities that reflect proficiency. This is related both to limitations of task, which will be dealt with later on in this chapter, as well as to the range of contexts that instructors work within and across. The last area explored concerns the descriptive nature of the CLB and the extent to which the connections between task performance and description of abilities are interpretive in nature. This interpretation is mediated through multiple factors for teachers, including individual experiences and the contextual constraints in which they teach.

The descriptive quality in the CLB is defined as a continuum of development, a concept well aligned with research and theory in second-language acquisition, and intuitively comfortable for teachers who are in a position to see dynamic change in their learners and appreciate how much this varies across individuals and contexts. In terms of assessment, however, it presents certain challenges: in using the document for assessment, the concept of the continuum becomes difficult to reconcile with the realities of the classroom. The continuum is conceptualized along a set of benchmarks intended to help teachers describe change in proficiency. In order to document movement from one level to another, there must be points along the continuum that will act to some degree as discrete points. Programs with clearly defined levels rely on assessment that is discrete in outcome, if not in process, so that the levels are clear to learners and instructors. In describing how learners progress though the benchmarks, the document notes "lateral development and progress within a benchmark" (CIC and CCLB 2012, xii). It further notes that the ways proficiency is described, with terms such as "fluent," are intended to describe "a degree of ability within a stage ... not an absolute descriptor of discourse. ... It means that a learner has reached a successful degree of ability in the types of tasks and at the level of demand associated with a particular stage of the CLB" (x). Learners at a CLB 4 level, for example, are therefore functioning within that benchmark, and will be at various points along the continuum with respect to the range of skills and knowledge that characterize that benchmark. In the classroom, this is not problematic, in that a learner centred pedagogy allows learners to develop at their pace within a range of proficiency. It becomes challenging when teachers are required to plan instruction and test outcomes in order to "move" learners across levels within a program. In a program of instruction, when students complete CLB 4, they are moved to CLB 5 with the understanding that they will begin learning the competences of the new level. However, when a learner arrives for the first time in a program, if the placement of CLB 4 is interpreted as a test result, the learner would logically be placed in CLB 5. As if in acknowledgement of the need to clarify interpretation of CLB assessment, the *National Language Placement and Progression Guidelines* issued by CIC in 2013 state that an assigned benchmark indicates that "the learner has achieved, and demonstrated, the level of communicative ability associated with **most or all** (traditionally, 70 to 100 percent) of the descriptors for the benchmarks assigned in each of the four skills" (CIC 2013, 3). In fact, a learner may be able to perform some tasks at one or two benchmarks higher or lower than the one assigned.

Context, as described in the CLB, plays a prominent role in helping teachers assess proficiency. It is described across the three stages as non-demanding, moderately demanding, and demanding, characterized as basic, familiar, and high-stakes. Likewise, the complexity of language is described as simple, moderately complex, and complex. This language is vague and difficult to interpret and demands an acceptance of highly nuanced perspectives that are aligned with a dynamic perspective of development, but poses difficulties when looking for how to judge the appropriateness of materials or tasks. "Demanding" is also a reflection of ability, yet it seems here that the quality is being judged as normative, though it is unclear against what norm, while "simplicity" and "complexity" are dependent on purpose of task, where language may need to be simple in some tasks and more complex in others. Profiles of ability use descriptive language to illustrate how learners may differ in the way they use language. Knowledge and strategies indicate abilities that need to be "acquired" in order to "achieve a benchmark." This is where the CLB become a tool for assessment, and it underscores the impact of assessment on teaching. The suggestion here is that the learner can "acquire" specific abilities, which can be assessed at particular levels, so the teacher can teach specific abilities in order to help learners attain those levels.

A second focal point of this section, the notion of task, is central to the CLB. They are designed to capture purposeful communication and provide the basis for assessment. Description of an individual's proficiency is expressed in terms of the person's ability to perform a task, one that provides "demonstrable and measurable performance outcomes" (CIC 2013, ix). The use of tasks as tools of measurement poses challenges. A critical dimension of task as measurement is a consideration of "features of communication"; however, this includes an attempt to quantify change. Fox and Courchêne (2005) reviewed the CLB 2000 and noted several key features of this version, including the incongruencies stemming from an effort to measure progression through tasks by, for example, using text length to show progression in writing from one benchmark to another. They further note disparities such as an increase from providing a three- to four-paragraph text at CLB 8 to writing a four- to five-page essay at CLB 9.

While Fox and Courchêne (2005) wrote about the 2000 version, the same challenges are found in the current document (CIC CLB 2012). When we examine the development of speaking skills, dialogues are described in terms of length (two turns at CLB 1, four turns at CLB 2, six at CLB 3, and eight at CLB 4), while speech is described as ranging from "clear and at a slow rate" (CLB 1) to "clear and at a slow to normal rate" (CLB 4). Rate of speech, however, is highly dependent on a range of purposes, such as context and individual factors, not captured in these descriptions. In other examples, at CLB 4 writers are expected to produce seven sentences in the context of business or service messages, but one paragraph when writing for the purpose of sharing information about an event or experience. Presentations at speaking CLB 5 are up to five minutes long, at CLB 6 they are up to seven minutes, at CLB 7 they are up to ten minutes long, and at CLB 8 they are up to twenty minutes long, yet they all require connected discourse and are delivered in a context that is "moderately demanding." Teachers need to interpret these criteria – especially as they are used for assessment – relative to the learners they work with and their teaching contexts, as well as their own teaching experience across both contexts and groups of learners; thus, it is worth exploring how teachers themselves think about the CLB in relation to their teaching practice.

2. A Framework for Instruction

The findings of the national consultation included an in-depth look at appropriate support for teachers using CLB (Smit and Turcot 2010).

The first important finding was the correlation between the length of time teachers had been working with the CLB and their levels of knowledge and satisfaction with their ability to use the CLB (32). Specifically, instructors with ten or more years of experience (even five or more years) rated their satisfaction at 9 or 10 out of a possible 10. However, the majority of instructors with less than a year's experience rated their satisfaction with their abilities using the CLB lower than 5. The role of experience in engendering teacher confidence and comfort in using CLB is an important element in considering the variable experiences of teachers with the CLB. However, teachers working with the Benchmarks also have a wide range of training: from no training at all to college and university-based TESL certificates, and all the way up to graduate degrees in Applied Linguistics. Working with provincially accredited teachers, Faez and Valeo (2012) investigated the degree to which TESL program graduates felt prepared to implement the CLB. They found that on a scale of 1 to 10, the mean response was 7, without significant variation across programs. Survey data with teachers of ESL to adults, however, have shown enormous variation in working contexts and conditions, including full-time unionized positions and part-time contract positions (see Haque and Cray 2007, Valeo 2013, Valeo and Faez 2013). Thus, not only the number of years of teaching experience, but also teaching context and training are significant factors in levels of teacher confidence and comfort with the CLB.

Back in 1997, Fleming interviewed instructors about the CLB and found that although most teachers were positive about the Benchmarks, they still had concerns about how this might impact their curricular autonomy, especially regarding selection of teaching materials (Fleming 1998). In the years since, CLB-informed LINC (Language Instruction for Newcomers to Canada) curriculum guidelines and teaching materials have been created, and these are now commonly used in most adult immigrant language training programs. In this way, almost all programs now draw on CLB to provide the backbone for curriculum development; nonetheless, there is still considerable program variation in how these curricula are developed and implemented in the classroom. Specifically, teachers continue to want to structure their own needs assessments and classroom activities in order to be able to respond to variable learner needs, even as the Benchmarks have become a central reference point for LINC teachers, structuring what is taught and how it is taught (Haque and

Cray 2010). In his research on the development and implementation of the CLB-informed LINC 4 and 5 curriculum guidelines, Pinet (2006) found that the CLB framework does not significantly restrict teachers' autonomy in curricular planning; however, other researchers have found that if curriculum guidelines are left too widely open to interpretation, this may lead to confusion in curricular planning (Haque and Cray 2010, Melles 2008).

In order to examine the question of how the Benchmarks inform teachers' curriculum planning and teaching practice, in this section we draw on interview material – some previously published in Haque and Cray (2010) and some not – with twenty-five LINC instructors (in levels ranging from Literacy to LINC 5), conducted one-on-one, in a moderately sized Ontario city that receives a large number of newcomers every year. All interviewees had TESL certification and university degrees, with a range of classroom experience from novice to over twenty years of TESL. Interviewees were approached through snowball sampling and taught in a wide range of programs, including those run by school boards, colleges, community organizations, and private schools; therefore, some teachers worked in well-resourced institutional contexts with colleagues and program co-ordinators on site, while others worked in isolated physical spaces not designed for teaching, including portables, church basements, and "classrooms" under gyms.

What immediately became clear during the interviews was that teachers were all aware of the central importance of the CLB for guiding both the teaching and the assessment of their learners. The importance of the Benchmarks had been impressed upon teachers, not only through CIC directives and local and regional conferences/workshops, but also by local program co-ordinators and supporting instruction documentation. Instructors' acknowledgement of the importance of Benchmarks was consistently captured in such statements as, "You have to use the Benchmarks" and "We have all fallen in line" [with the Benchmarks] (Haque and Cray 2010, 72). Where teachers were less consistent in their responses was when they discussed *how* the Benchmarks were to be used.

Many teachers began by outlining how they used the Benchmarks for in-class assessment. Although initial placement assessment is done externally, and ideally all learners arrive with a set of four Benchmark levels (for speaking, writing, reading, and listening), once enrolled in class, instructors must assess learners in order to chart learner progress and also to determine when the learner can move into the next class level. Many teachers use the Benchmarks, with their detailed competency tables and profiles of ability, to guide these in-class assessments. For example, one instructor stated, "The Benchmarks themselves are an outcome based test," and another teacher echoed, "The Benchmarks are only the skills that you can test" (Haque and Cray 2010, 72). In this way, the Benchmarks were used as set learning objectives to be mastered and subsequently assessed. The centrality of the CLB was also felt as teachers tried to determine if learners were ready to move to the next LINC level; specifically, teachers needed to find ways to assess their learners' proficiency through Benchmark-based reports. One teacher described using assessments calibrated to Benchmarks in order to "justify placements." The CLB-based resource that instructors mentioned most often when talking about assessment was the CLB *Can Do Statements* (CCLB 2014), as these provided the most direct way to assess if learners were able to do what they were expected to do at their level. As an echo to many such comments, one teacher stated, "The Can Do's are the easiest way for me to make sure I'm keeping to the CLB."

Although the detailed competency tables and profiles of ability provided useful standards for assessment, not all teachers believed that the CLB enabled precise assessments. As one instructor explained, students in her particular level did not exactly fit the learner profile implicit in the CLB level descriptors, and this meant that she had to reinterpret the objectives to fit the class. Another instructor stated that the Benchmarks were not particularly relevant for her learners' needs, so she managed assessment by "doing it backwards." Specifically, she first ascertained the level at which her learners should be placed, then she would "plug in the Benchmarks that is [sic] going to get them into the class where I think they fit" (Haque and Cray 2010, 72). In this way, the CLB regulated the continuum along which learners were assessed and the measures that marked student progress in language training. Therefore, by establishing and placing the learning objectives against which student progress was measured, the CLB served a curricular function for teaching and assessment, with instructors inevitably "teaching to" the Benchmarks.

The CLB figured significantly in how instructors organized in-class assessments; they also served to structure what was taught and how. Some instructors gleaned themes from the CLB Sample Tasks, using them as "guidelines" around which they could organize their lesson plans and teaching activities. As well, the CLB provided guidelines for the teaching of skills, particularly through the organizational layout, which was based on the four skills of listening, speaking, reading, and writing. As one instructor explained, "I try to be sure that Benchmarks are covered in the reading, writing and speaking part of it. ... I do make sure that I do stay within those guidelines" (73). She added that "depending on the [student] needs, you might have to fudge around with Benchmarks a bit." Still, instructors found that the CLB provided a "good foundation," and another instructor explained her close use of Benchmarks this way: "I set my outcome according to the outcomes in the guidelines and that is what I am working towards when I am making my lesson plans" (73).

Instructors had varied opinions about both the importance and the method of grammar instruction in their classrooms. However, they were all keenly aware that grammar instruction was something they needed to do in their classes, especially given the specification of "grammatical knowledge" at the start of each skills section in the CLB. For example, each of the CLB skills sections lists a set of "things that may need to be learned as an individual moves through Stage 1 [or II or III] Reading [or Listening or Speaking or Writing]." Items listed under grammatical knowledge include knowledge of such things as "simple and continuous verb tenses, simple modals" (CIC 2013, 75) or "past conditionals, past or future perfect, passive subordinate adverbial clauses" (99), and so on. Teachers cited these types of specifications in the CLB as part of their awareness of the importance of grammar instruction in LINC classes. One instructor stated that since she taught a LINC 2 level, she felt that students needed explicit instruction on verb tenses, prepositions, and basic sentence structure, and another teacher echoed her call, stating "If they [learners] don't have good grammar, they don't speak well or write well and so we tend to emphasize grammar" (Haque and Clay, 76).

Instructors did not all agree as to how grammar instruction should proceed, with some teachers stating that they built their grammar instruction into their lesson content or instruction themes, and others outlining the need for and importance of explicit grammar instruction. For example, one teacher described how she integrated modals into her lesson theme on housing through an activity that was designed around looking for an apartment, because modals "fit in with the theme" (76). Another instructor determined what grammar points learners should be learning at their level by checking the Benchmarks to see, "Is it reported speech at this point or is it just asking questions?" (76). Many instructors also felt that explicit grammar instruction was important; one teacher explained, "I think that the grammar is important and you can never get too good in grammar," therefore explicit instruction is important, since "the grammar might get lost in the themes. I like to keep them separate." (76). Finally, there was a group of instructors who would introduce a grammatical concept through their thematic teaching content and then would "apply that grammar" through repeated focused activities. Thus, the CLB created an awareness of the importance of grammar instruction for teachers, but the CLB's lack of direction (in contrast to what might be specified in a curriculum) as to how grammar instruction should proceed meant that instructors used a range of methods for bringing grammar instruction into the classroom.

The CLB also guided how teachers filled out their monthly reports, which were how their institutions – community organizations, school boards, private schools, and others – reported to CIC, which in turn used these reports in part to monitor the programs and allocate/renew funding. Almost all teachers we interviewed had to fill out monthly reports on what they had taught, and these reports were based on the Benchmarks, in that they indexed skills, materials, and activities to the CLB descriptors. As one instructor stated, "I don't know if mine [the monthly report] is helpful, but I realize that the bosses have to account for what they are doing" (73). A second teacher elaborated, "Monthly, they ask us to do a report about what happened in the class in terms of our performance outcomes and our teaching objectives for the month. ... That shows whatever we have done in class for that month. I do the usual reading and writing for the month" (73). Another instructor confirmed that these monthly reports served not only as a monitor for CIC but also a way to ensure that teachers used the Benchmarks. Some teachers also confirmed that they referred to the CLB mainly when they were writing up their reports and not as much for developing lesson plans, as they felt that the Benchmarks' objectives were not necessarily appropriate for their learners' needs. This tied into a common thread in the interviews, particularly with experienced teachers. They often reported that they had a better understanding of their learners' needs and could draw on their professional training and experience to determine best what was useful and appropriate for their learners. These teachers stated that their experience and training meant they often trusted their "gut feelings" over the Benchmarks when determining what their students needed for language learning, and what they should be able to do at their level. As one teacher explained, "I have been here for fifteen years and I know what I'm doing" (75).

It is clear that teachers in adult immigrant language training programs have an extensive awareness of the Benchmarks. Furthermore, the CLB have a significant influence on how teachers develop curriculum and teaching content for their classes as well as how teachers think about their teaching. Nonetheless, despite the influence of the CLB, it is also clear that teachers have their own thoughts about the extent to which the Benchmarks are useful for their teaching practice. One common concern teachers expressed was that the Benchmarks did not fit the profile of their learners: some learners already possess the skills and knowledge that are specified to be taught at their level, and other learners may need skills and knowledge that are not identified in their Benchmark level. This problem extends to assessment, where instructors often feel that they are basing their assessments on descriptors that they do not believe fully reflect what their students need to learn or have learned (Haque and Cray 2010, 74). Although the CLB state clearly in the introduction that they are a set of descriptors and not a curriculum, the lack of specificity around how to translate these descriptors into the classroom also meant that instructors had a wide range in their interpretation of the Benchmarks for classroom practice, even if they didn't completely believe that Benchmarks were fully applicable to their teaching context. One instructor summarized the Benchmarks this way, "What a pain ... ", and another elaborated, "The Benchmarks still need some work. You have to read an enormous amount of claptrap in order to understand what you need" (75).

This broad range of understandings and interpretations, as well as the amount of informational material that needs to be understood by instructors, indicates the importance of support and training for teachers. As the final report on the national consultation on the CLB 2000 detailed, teachers identified a variety of supports that would help them in applying the CLB to their teaching contexts. Over 80 percent of instructors identified supports, such as workshops on developing skills to apply the CLB, sharing and problem solving among practitioners working in the same organization, and having formal training on the CLB, including orientations to the CLB; and over 90 percent of instructors wanted resources that would provide models and tools to help them apply the CLB (Smit and Turcot 2010, 33–34). Although there are already supports in place, which some teachers have access to, particular kinds of support – which many teachers identified as very beneficial – were not available to between 50 and 75 percent of teachers; these included e-learning or on-site mentoring, on-site training by outside professionals, and formal training on the CLB (34). Given the importance of training for effective use of the CLB, many instructors commented on this lack of access, "The lack of training results in people not understanding and they don't buy-in and don't use the CLB," and, "There is a huge difference between the amount of training being provided to users of the CLB" (35). Instructors were clear about what they would like to see in terms of training and support, "I would like on-site delivery of training because of the uniqueness of so many programs but also because there would be a mentor with ongoing involvement," and, "Instructors are at different levels of understanding of the CLB. Award a certificate in CLB. It is even more important than a TESL certificate" (35). Thus, given the wide range of teachers and their needs, practitioners called for a national standard in CLB-implementation support that would include training to build and retain competencies in the CLB through orientation and ongoing informal and formal training, along with mentoring, peer support, and access to required resources (Smit and Turcot, 2010).

Lack of consistency in access to training also meant that there were calls for more CLB-focused pre-service training, and enforcement of these standards through program-certification bodies such as TESL Canada and TESL Ontario. The CCLB and other service delivery organizations were called upon to ensure provision, support, and access to CLB-related training – both nationally and in-house – and funders were asked to also adequately fund professional development. As instructors commented, "We need a national strategy to train teachers. CCLB needs to take a stronger role in making that happen," and, "If the cost barrier would be removed, a lot more teachers would get training. I am the only one in my organization who takes workshops. I am punished because my time is not paid for" (Smit and Turcot 2010, 36). Thus, the development of a national training framework specifying best practices for adequately funded pre-service and in-service supports for the CLB implementation was a priority for many practitioners.

Finally, practitioners commented on the importance of CLB-related resources for their language-teaching support. Between 50 and 75 percent of teachers mentioned the importance of resources from the CCLB main website, including the CLB theoretical framework, among others, and the most highly rated resource identified by teachers was the CLB *Can Do* checklists/statements (Smit and Turcot 2010, 37). Instructors were also specific in identifying exactly what kinds of resources and materials would help them best to implement CLB-informed language training. By far the top identified resources (90 percent) were those that could be used directly to inform classroom teaching. These included both print and audio-visual sample tasks/exemplars, CLB-based classroom-ready materials, and CLB-based curriculum model/s (37). Although there are a host of support materials available, such as the LINC curriculum guidelines, as well as many published support textbooks and materials, teacher demand for new and CLB-based materials is ongoing, given the challenges of CLB implementation and often limited time/support for material and resource development.

3. The Canadian Language Benchmarks and Teachers: Moving Forward

The national consultation report outlined what stakeholders identified as gaps, needs, and challenges related to implementing the CLB. While there was variation across Canada, a number of common areas emerged and led to the articulation of a critical question: "Are the CLB [and the NCLC] frameworks or [are they] standards for understanding and measuring language proficiency, or both?" (Smit and Turcot 2010, 18). Indeed, as a framework, the CLB will help teachers work with the strengths and challenges learners bring to the newcomer classroom experience. As a standard, the CLB can support placement in the programs and classrooms that will provide the most appropriate instruction. Recommendations emerging from the consultation highlighted the need to "enhance rigour" to support the CLB as a standard, including greater distinction in how the levels are differentiated, clearer descriptors, increased "capacity to track outcomes and differences between outcomes across levels" (22), and a clearer rationale for the twelve-point scale. However, it is in the detailed responses from the instructors of adult immigrant language training programs that we can see exactly how the CLB informs assessment and classroom practice, how teachers interpret the CLB, and therefore what exactly the remaining gaps, challenges, and needs are for implementing the CLB.

It is clear that the CLB provide a clear range of descriptors; however, the importance of context, particularly for assessment, cannot be emphasized enough. This is particularly true in the implementation of tasks as tools for measurement and in interpreting the complexities of individual learner characteristics and language-skill abilities in relation to a continuum of descriptors of proficiency. Even as the lack of specificity in the descriptors is a strength of the CLB, this lack also means that instructors often have a wide range in their interpretations of the CLB for both assessment and their classroom practice. Although instructors have a high degree of awareness about the CLB and acknowledge the importance of the CLB for guiding their teaching and assessment, their interpretation and implementation of the CLB for these purposes is highly dependent on their training and experience. This becomes clear in their discussions of how the CLB informs their assessment of learners, and in how they develop instructional content – including grammar teaching content – as well as how they report on these activities in their monthly reports. However, most instructors still want further support, including both pre-service and in-service training, mentoring, and specific resources to help guide them in the use of the CLB to inform their teaching and assessment. Since the development of the first CLB in 1996, each successive edition has identified and attempted to respond to gaps and challenges that emerged through practice. While a sound theoretical framework is essential, it is also critical that the process of renewal continue to draw on the classroom and the experiences of instructors, who ultimately give the CLB the greatest purpose.

References

Centre for Canadian Language Benchmarks. 2014. *Can Do Statements*. Ottawa: Centre for Canadian Language Benchmarks.

Chui, Tina. 2003. *Longitudinal Survey of Immigrants to Canada: Process, Progress and Prospects*. Ottawa: Statistics Canada. Accessed May 30, 2016. http://www.statcan.gc.ca/pub/89-611-x/89-611-x2003001-eng.pdf?contentType=application%2Fpdf.

Citizenship and Immigration Canada, and Centre for Canadian Language Benchmarks. 2012. *Canadian Language Benchmarks: English as a second language for adults*. Ottawa: Citizenship and Immigration Canada.

Citizenship and Immigration Canada. 2013. *National Language Placement and Progression Guidelines*. Ottawa: Citizenship and Immigration Canada.

Faez, Farahnaz, and Antonella Valeo. 2012. "TESOL teacher education: Novice teachers' perceptions of their preparedness and efficacy in the classroom." *TESOL Quarterly* 46(3): 450–470.

Fleming, Douglas. 1998. "Autonomy and agency in curriculum decision-making: A study of instructors in a Canadian adult settlement ESL program." *TESL Canada Journal* 16(1): 19–35.

Fox, Janna, and Robert Courchêne. 2005. "The Canadian Language Benchmarks (CLB): A critical appraisal." *Contact: Research Symposium Issue* 31(2): 7–29.

Haque, Eve, and Ellen Cray. 2010. "LINC-ing policy and practice in the immigrant language training classroom." *Contact: Research Symposium Issue* 36(2): 68–83.

———. 2007. "Constraining teachers: Adult ESL settlement language training policy." *TESOL Quarterly* 41(3): 634–642.

Holmes, Tara. 2005. *Integrating CLB assessment into your ESL classroom*. Ottawa: Citizenship and Immigration Canada.

Melles, Gavin. 2008. "Curriculum documents and practice in the NZ polytechnic sector: consensus and dissensus." *Research in Post-Compulsory Education* 13(1): 55–67.

Pinet, Ron. 2006. "The contestation of citizenship education at three stages of the LINC 4 & 5 curriculum guidelines: Production, reception, and implementation." *TESL Canada Journal* 24(1): 1–20.

Smit, Pamela, and Paul Turcot. 2010. *National Consultation on the Canadian Language Benchmarks 2000 and Niveaux de competence linguistique canadiens 2006: Final report*. Ottawa: Citizenship and Immigration Canada.

Valeo, Antonella. 2013. "The TESL Ontario member survey: A brief report." *Contact* 39(1): 54–58. Accessed May 30, 2016. http://www.teslontario.net/uploads/publications/contact/ContactSpring2011.pdf.

Valeo, Antonella, and Farahnaz Faez. 2013. "Career development and professional attrition of novice ESL teachers." *TESL Canada Journal* 31(1): 1–19.

Wette, Rosemary. 2009. "Making the instructional curriculum as an interactive, contextualized process: case studies of seven ESOL teachers." *Language Teaching Research* 13(4): 337–365.

CHAPTER 4

Teaching and Assessment: Using the CLB in a Range of Contexts under the Stewardship of the Centre for Canadian Language Benchmarks

Anne Senior
ASTEC Inc., Specialist Consultant to CCLB

1. Introduction

This chapter outlines the evolution and expanding focus of the *Canadian Language Benchmarks* (CLB) and describes the many tools and resources developed by the Centre for Canadian Language Benchmarks (CCLB) to support the use of the CLB as a practical, fair, reliable, and transparent national standard for assessing, teaching, and evaluating English as a second language in Canada. The CCLB also developed and revised the *Niveaux de compétence linguistique canadiens* (NCLC) and continues to support their use as a practical, fair, reliable, and transparent national standard for assessing, teaching, and evaluating French as a second language in Canada. The development and use of the NCLC are covered in another chapter of this book; this chapter focuses on the CLB.

The chapter begins with a brief review of, and rationale for, the evolution of the CLB in relation to assessment, teaching, and evaluation. It continues by examining the role of the CCLB in the evolution of the CLB and in the safeguarding of the standard. The chapter then reviews the CLB as they are used for placement assessment, high-stakes assessment, tool and resource development, teacher training, and employment. It concludes by considering the future of the CLB and the CCLB.

2. Evolution of the Canadian Language Benchmarks

The *Canadian Language Benchmarks* are the national standard for describing, measuring, and recognizing the English-language proficiency of persons in Canada, as well as of immigrants and other persons destined for Canada (CCLB 2016a). Since 1996, they have become the backbone of Canada's publicly-funded adult second-language training programs. To support and promote their use as a practical, fair, reliable, and transparent national standard, the CCLB was established in 1998.

The CLB, including a literacy component, were developed in 1996 by the federal department then known as Citizenship and Immigration Canada (CIC), in response to a need articulated by new immigrants in 1993 at the Teachers of English as a Second Language (TESL) Canada Learners' Conference. The learners sought a way of enabling themselves to demonstrate and understand their language proficiency and to help them access the services, supports, and jobs that they needed in order to settle in Canada. Responding to this need, the CLB were developed for use in Canada within publicly funded language training and assessment organizations. As awareness and use of the CLB grew over the years, additional uses for the standard were recognized. The CLB were primarily established with a settlement focus, but employment and economic needs, wider use of the CLB with other types of programming, and the addition of higher-level and targeted language training led to the expanded use of the standard in a variety of second-language contexts.

Revisions to the CLB were made in 2000 and 2012 (Pawlikowska-Smith 2000, CIC and CCLB 2012) in response to evolving needs and changes in foci. The 2012 version incorporated a high degree of rigour, which was confirmed by a comprehensive validation process (Burnot-Trites and Barbour 2012). This revision supported the use of the CLB in contexts where they had been previously found deficient, such as academic, employment, and overseas applications. The CLB are now recognized as appropriate for use in a wide variety of contexts, including high-stakes ones. These include language training, assessment, immigration, and citizenship, as well as workplace, regulatory, and academic contexts. Enshrined in the *Immigration and Refugee Protection Act* (IRPA) regulations, the CLB have unified discussion among diverse stakeholders across the country on topics such as the development of tools and resources, performance measurement, immigrant selection policy, and citizenship goals (Blakely and Singh 2012).

Although there was a version of the CLB for literacy in the 1996 document, it was in 2000 that, recognizing the diverse needs of learners, the government of Manitoba co-founded the development of the *Canadian Language Benchmarks 2000: ESL for Literacy Learners* (CIC 2000), which laid out the progression of reading, writing, and numeracy skills for English as a second language (ESL) adult learners with limited or no literacy skills, and which could also be used with ESL students who were literate in a non-Roman alphabet but who needed to learn reading and writing basics in English. In 2014, that document was comprehensively revised to more closely align the literacy benchmarks with those of the new CLB. The *Canadian Language Benchmarks: ESL for ALL (Adult Literacy Learners)* (CIC and CCLB 2014) is an updated, comprehensive document designed to support program administrators, curriculum developers, teachers, and assessors in the instruction of ESL learners who have limited or no literacy skills.

3. Why Did this Evolution Occur?

The CLB consist of twelve benchmarks in three stages that describe language proficiency from the very beginning to advanced levels of proficiency. The standard has a solid theoretical framework, reflecting the communicative models of language ability promoted by Bachman (1990), Bachman and Palmer (1996, 2010), and Celce-Murcia, Dörnyei and Thurrell (1995). According to Bachman (1990), language ability requires a combination of language knowledge (i.e., knowledge of grammatical, lexical, organizational, and pragmatic rules of language use) and strategic competence (cognitive and meta-cognitive strategies for managing language knowledge). The CLB competency statements reflect the inter-relationship of constituent aspects of language ability that can be demonstrated through language tasks. The CLB are task-based and learner-centred (CIC and CCLB 2012).

The solid theoretical framework (Burnot-Trites et al. 2015), revision, and comprehensive validation process (Burnot-Trites and Barbour, 2012) ensured that the 2012 version of the CLB could be compared with, and hold up well against, other international standards, such as the *Common European Framework of Reference* (CEFR) (Council of Europe, 2001). Thus the CCLB can reference independent validation experts and reviewers when it says:

> The CLB can be used for a variety of purposes, including adult ESL programming and instruction, proficiency assessment, curriculum and resource development, test design, and occupational benchmarking, among others. The CLB help the professional field of adult ESL articulate language learning needs, best practices, and accomplishments. For learners, the CLB provide a basis for understanding how their language abilities are placed within the continuum of overall language competence. The CLB can also assist them in setting personal language learning goals, developing learning plans, monitoring their progress, and adjusting their language learning strategies to achieve their goals. The CLB are used by instructors to identify learners' language competence in order to develop program content that is relevant and meaningful to learners. The CLB inform language instruction and provide a common framework for assessing learner progress that will facilitate movement from one level to another. Language assessors use the CLB to articulate the language abilities of adult ESL learners so that they are placed in suitable programs. Assessments based on the CLB facilitate the portability of ESL learners' credentials, as well as their movement between classes or programs, across provinces and territories, or between post-secondary institutions. (CIC and CCLB 2012, v)

Moreover, test developers use the CLB to create assessment tools to measure and report on learner proficiency levels for a variety of purposes and stakeholders, and benchmarking experts use the CLB to compare the language demands of an occupation to particular levels of proficiency to help various stakeholders (e.g., labour-market associations, sector councils, licensing bodies, and employers) understand how the language requirements for specific professions and trades are referenced to the national standard of language proficiency, and, in some cases, determine correlation to existing occupational task-based standards.

4. Role of the CCLB in this Evolution

Addressing the needs of English as a second language and literacy practitioners are key activities for the CCLB, which is the centre of expertise in support of both the CLB and the NCLC national standards. Soon after the introduction of the CLB in 1996, the need emerged for an institution outside government to take responsibility for CLB projects. Key federal and provincial funders and other stakeholders co-operated to establish the CCLB, so in March 1998 the CCLB received its charter as a non-profit corporation.

The CCLB's mission is to lead and provide expertise in the implementation and dissemination of the CLB as a practical, fair, and reliable national standard of English-language proficiency, in education, training, community, and workplace settings. This chapter relates to CCLB's support of the CLB; however, its roles and responsibilities are equally applicable to the NCLC.

The CCLB's current strategic plan states its five key directions, which are consistent with the intent behind its establishment in 1998 (CCLB 2015):

- Develop and share quality resources associated with the CLB
- Develop additional assessment processes and tools
- Develop new resources to support language teaching/learning
- Apply the CLB to support successful labour-market integration
- Refine organizational capacity to further the Centre's leadership role

As mentioned earlier, the CCLB maintains a comprehensive national CLB assessment system for use in adult ESL, education, training, and the labour market. It also provides a system of recognition for assessors and assessment service providers across Canada. With the support of federal and provincial funders, the CCLB has also developed numerous tools and resources to support assessors and practitioners, and has collaborated or advised on many others.

Nowadays, all of Immigration, Refugees and Citizenship Canada's (IRCC's) language tools and resources are based on the CLB framework, ensuring consistency and reliability. The catalyst for much of the CCLB's work is the federal government's Language Instruction for Newcomers to Canada (LINC) program, which was introduced in 1992. The LINC program made official-language training available to all adult permanent residents, with over 100,000 learners participating in the program in 2015. Although LINC is primarily classroom-based, LINC Home Study was developed in 1995 to provide a distance-training option for newcomers who otherwise would have no access to language training. LINC Home Study has evolved from a largely correspondence model to a largely online system.

LINC programming is accessed through a comprehensive, national, CLB-based assessment system. Although this chapter focuses on CLB-related tools and resources, it is impossible to discuss assessment and assessor training without acknowledging the pioneering and ongoing work of the Peel Board of Education's Centre for Language Training and Assessment (CLTA) – later The Centre for Education and Training (TCET) – and the contribution of test developers Bonny Peirce and Gail Stewart, who developed many CLB-based assessments for both the TCET and the CCLB.

In announcing its new immigrant language training policy in the early 1990s, Employment and Immigration Canada (a predecessor of IRCC) stressed that a key to developing the most effective training possible is to clearly relate the training to individual needs of clients. It stated that to do this, "reliable tools are needed to measure the language skills possessed by clients against standard language proficiency criteria. For federally-funded training this will mean that real client language needs can be met and that clients will have access to equivalent types and results of training regardless of where they settle in Canada" (Rogers 1993, 1). This policy had significant influence on the development of placement-assessment tools that are used nationally. These tools provide a portable credential for placement into appropriate language training and inform curriculum development, materials, and resources.

5. The CLB and Placement Assessment

The CLB standardized assessment tools have been developed and validated for achievement, placement, or outcomes testing that either assessors or instructors in ESL classes can administer under rigorous test conditions to produce reliable results. Standardized assessor training, as well as calibration and refresher workshops, are a mandatory part of accreditation to conduct CLB-based placement assessments, which helps to maintain consistency and fairness of administration.

For initial placement in language programs, learners are assessed by tests which assign benchmarks that indicate the degree of ability the learner achieves for each language skill. In order to be assigned a benchmark, a learner must demonstrate the abilities and characteristics of that benchmark to a sufficient degree. The development of the first version of the CLB and the first placement test, the *Canadian Language*

Benchmarks Assessment (CLBA), took place concurrently and iteratively (Norton Peirce and Stewart 1997). The CLBA was developed under the direction of the Peel Board of Education. Both the 1996 CLB working document and the test separated language skills into three distinct areas: listening/speaking, reading, and writing.

The revised version of the CLB published in 2000 separated language skills into four distinct areas: listening, speaking, reading, and writing. The need to assess the four skills independently, instead of combining listening and speaking, and the desire for a more streamlined assessment, led to the CCLB developing the *Canadian Language Benchmarks Placement Test* (CLBPT) in 2002. The CLBA and the CLBPT are both still used across Canada on a face-to-face basis for placement into language training programs and are usually administered through assessment centres. There are multiple versions of both tests, but neither one has undergone significant revision after the publication of the 2012 version of the CLB. In 2015, the CCLB adapted the CLBPT for remote delivery as a viable alternative to using itinerant assessors and to increase client access using non-traditional means.

The *Canadian Language Benchmarks Literacy Assessment* (CLBLA) was created in 2000 to support the placement of literacy learners into programs using the CLB. The *Literacy Placement Tool* (LPT) volumes 1 and 2 followed in 2005. The two tests are very different. Developed for use by trained assessors, the CLBLA uses learners' first-language tasks in twenty-six languages to determine what literacy skills they have that would be transferable to the acquisition of English as a second language. LPT volumes 1 and 2 were developed for use by ESL literacy assessors and practitioners to facilitate appropriate placement in a literacy program and assessment within the program. The LPT assessment is conducted only in English. Although both tests are somewhat compatible with the CLB 2000 literacy document (even though the CLBLA is based on the 1996 version of the CLB), a new test shall be developed in order to take into account the increased knowledge of the literacy learners' needs that is reflected in the *Canadian Language Benchmarks: ESL for ALL* 2014 version.

Recognizing that language proficiency may be a driver for successful employment, both the CCLB and the TCET have also developed tests to assess learners with higher-level benchmarks in order to facilitate entry into bridging programs or specialized language training. These assessments: *Enhanced Language Training Placement Assessment* (ELTPA), developed by TCET, and *Workplace*

Language Assessment (WLA) (CCLB 2009), developed by the CCLB, assess up to CLB levels 9/10.

All the assessments mentioned above are key components of Immigration, Refugees and Citizenship Canada's (IRCC's) *National Language Placement and Progression Guidelines* (CIC 2013), with data recorded in the Immigration Contribution Agreement Reporting Environment (iCARE); the History of Assessments, Referrals and Training system (HARTs); and IRCC's and the Ontario Ministry of Citizenship, Immigration and International Trade's Co-ordinated Language Assessment and Referral System (CLARS).

The CCLB and the TCET developed assessments separately throughout the early years of the CLB, as tools were seemingly funded on an ad hoc basis, in response to pressing and immediate demands. Recently, the two organizations have begun to develop tools collaboratively, capitalizing on their organizational strengths to be more cost- and time-effective, with less duplication. The maturation of the standard, along with increased awareness of the need for responsible stewardship and greater fiscal responsibility may be reflected in future collaborative approaches to test development.

6. The CLB and High-Stakes Assessment

In the early twenty-first century, the CCLB widened its range of test-development expertise with a move to occupation-specific and other high-stakes tests. The development and implementation of the *Canadian English Language Benchmark Assessment for Nurses* (CELBAN) meant that it was the first CLB-based test with the rigour and validity to be used for high-stakes purposes. It was also the first instance of a high-stakes assessment being used to assess language proficiency for a profession in North America.

The CELBAN was developed in 2004 by the CCLB in consultation with members of the nursing community and with input from regulatory bodies, associations, unions, and nursing refresher programs, as well as internationally educated nurses (IENs). It was designed to ease the nursing shortage in Canada by providing access to the pool of IENs who had arrived in Canada but had then encountered obstacles to obtaining employment. The CELBAN is an occupation-specific language test that assesses proficiency within real-world health care scenarios. It evaluates proficiency in listening, speaking, reading, and writing, and is now widely used and acknowledged as a key tool in assisting IENs' entry to practice in Canada. The CELBAN is one of two tests recognized as proof of language proficiency by all Canadian nursing regulators. The CCLB contracts the Touchstone Institute to act as the national CELBAN administration centre.

The CCLB also developed occupation-specific high-stakes tests in English and French for the engineering profession. Based on prior benchmarking research, these allowed for fair, valid, and reliable assessment for four engineering disciplines: civil, mechanical, electrical, and chemical. The development of these tests was significant, as both English and French versions of the test were developed simultaneously by a bilingual team of experts. These tests had not been implemented by Engineers Canada, owner of the tests, as of 2016.

The CCLB is playing an integral part in the ongoing global discussion and research on the relative value of occupation-specific tests versus generic high-stakes tests for determining the communicative competencies and language proficiency required to work successfully in regulated occupations.

In line with this debate, in 2010, CIC (now IRRC), contracted the CCLB to develop a prototype high-stakes generic assessment, the *Milestones* test, designed independently of language training programs to measure and certify proficiency from CLB 3 to 9+ levels. The *Milestones* test was designed to be especially rigorous at CLB 4 and CLB 7 levels. In 2015–16, it was used as one component of the LINC program evaluation to compare the language-learning progress of learners enrolled in LINC classes with that of individuals not enrolled in any language training.

The *Milestones* test has potential for use for a variety of high-stakes purposes, including citizenship, academic entry, and entry to practise within regulated professions. It is a highly secure, valid, and reliable standardized tool, with the flexibility to evolve based on future goals and needs.

The *Milestones* is the only high-stakes test in Canada that reflects specifically the CLB standard, and therefore should bring a high measure of confidence in its use as a valid, fair, and reliable assessment for purposes for which a CLB benchmark level is required.

7. The CLB Tools and Resources

While the CLB standard describes a broad range of competencies at each benchmark level, it is not a curriculum and does not include all the possible communication tasks learners may encounter or have to perform in their daily lives. The CCLB's development of additional task-based resources and tools, as well as training on how to use them, ensures that users of the standard are supported as they strive to meet their learners' needs.

One such resource is the *CLB Support Kit*, published by CCLB in 2012. Accompanied by exemplars of receptive and productive tasks at benchmarks 1 to 12, the *CLB Support Kit* was developed alongside the revised CLB 2012 to orient users to the new standard.

The kit serves as background information for in-service training on the revised CLB for instructors working in programs funded by IRCC. It includes exemplars for listening, speaking, reading, and writing for all CLB levels and is complemented by face-to-face training, often delivered using a train-the-trainer model.

A major initiative that will change the face of adult ESL training in Canada will be completely implemented by 2017–18: *Portfolio-Based Language Assessment* (PBLA) (Pettis 2014). In 2009, IRCC embarked on this journey through limited pilots in order to foster a formative assessment culture consistent with a CLB approach to teaching. When fully implemented, it is expected to motivate student progress and facilitate mobility among the CLB-based federal and provincial language training programs. PBLA is a comprehensive, systematic approach to language assessment in the classroom based on the model of Collaborative Language Assessment implemented in Manitoba in 2004. PBLA is intended to be embedded in curricula and should be an integral and ongoing part of the teaching and learning cycle. Depending on the CLB level, teachers and students collaborate to set language-learning goals, compile numerous examples of language proficiency and learning in a variety of contexts over time, analyse the data, and reflect on progress. PBLA was undertaken as an IRCC priority in response to studies on language training in Canada which noted that assessment in LINC programs was ad hoc and inconsistent (Makosky 2008, Nagy and Stewart 2009).

PBLA benefits both learners and instructors alike, as it addresses diagnostic, formative, and summative purposes of assessment and reflects research-based principles. PBLA motivates learners and engages them in their language learning, develops instructor expertise, and contributes to greater consistency in assessing and reporting on CLB outcomes. PBLA also contributes to the professional development of teachers and builds capacity. Teachers meet regularly in their own program, or with teachers in other programs, to ensure homogeneous and consistent implementation.

PBLA builds on a long tradition of CLB-based resources and tools supporting both formative and summative assessment: *Integrating CLB Assessment into your ESL Classroom* (Holmes 2005), *Summative Assessment Manual, CLB 5-10 Exit Assessment Tasks, Can Do Statements* (CCLB 2014), and *Can Do Statements for Employment* (CCLB 2016b). These tools and resources are available on the CCLB website (www.language.ca) and on Tutela (www.tutela.ca), the national online repository of language training resources. The CCLB co-ordinated and collected seed content for Tutela in the first phase of its development, and continues to support its vision of being a community of practice-driven initiatives for teachers to share resources and best practices, and to network with each other.

Learners may use a list of learning outcomes referenced to the CLB (such as the *Can Do Statements*) as a basis for self-assessment. Self-assessment provides valuable opportunities for learners to take greater responsibility for their own learning. It also allows them to reflect on their strengths and identify their goals. TCET has also developed an online self-assessment in English that corresponds with a similar tool developed by the CCLB in French to provide test-takers with an idea of their language ability.

The CLB owe their strength not only to the support they receive from the government of Canada but also to the provincial and territorial governments that have adopted them for adult ESL programming, and to the many service providers who use the CLB on a daily basis and who have also developed CLB-based tools and resources, often collaboratively with the CCLB. Support from Ontario's Ministry of Immigration, Citizenship and International Trade led to the development of *Quartz 2016: Ontario Curriculum Guidelines – interactive planning tools for course, unit lesson planning, and assessment*. To develop *Quartz*, the CCLB formed a partnership with the Toronto Catholic District School Board with the objective of aligning the Ontario language training program with the CLB and the *Niveaux de compétence linguistique canadiens* (NCLC).

8. The CLB and Teacher Training

The national consultation on the CLB, which published its report in 2010 (Smit and Turcot 2010), led to the revision of the standard in

2012, after receiving input from over 1,300 stakeholders. While overwhelmingly supportive of the CLB and its continued use, respondents indicated a continued need for training and support. The national consultation showed that there was disparity in terms of quality and quantity of CLB content available in TESL training programs for new ESL instructors, that instructors across the country valued and appreciated in-service training that they received on CLB tools and resources, and that CLB resources were very well respected and used in the field.

Nowadays, the CCLB offers professional development to support assessors and instructors, based on the theory of reflective practice that sees teachers as voluntary attendees who engage in professional development because they want to reflect on their practice in order to better serve their students (Farrell 2012). Training workshops are offered face-to-face and online across Canada, covering a range of topics based around the task-based approach and the theory of communicative competence.

For instance, funded in 2015–16 by the Ontario Ministry of Citizenship, Immigration and International Trade (MCIIT), the revised *CLB Boot Camp* is an online ten-hour self-study course on the revised *Canadian Language Benchmarks*. It comprises three modules: "CLB Basics," "Planning and the CLB," and "Assessment and the CLB." A certificate of completion can be generated for instructors wishing to document professional-development (PD) hours for TESL Ontario or for other purposes. This is an updated version of the original *CLB Boot Camp* developed in 2008.

In 2015, the government of Alberta funded a *CLB: ESL for ALL Boot Camp*, based on the new adult literacy standard that responds to needs articulated by literacy practitioners. This is an asynchronous training course that takes teachers through a structured learning cycle: orient, consider, apply, and reflect. The CCLB is proposing currently to develop more training on literacy, especially to support those working with literacy learners in mainstream classes.

Similar online and face-to-face training is an integral part of the sustainability plan for PBLA, to ensure that the transfer of knowledge is not diluted or undermined by lack of consistency.

Other CCLB resources support those working with learners with ESL literacy needs, with those preparing for the workplace, refugees, learners with higher levels of language, and general and occupation-specific workplace preparation needs. The CCLB also provides courses on the CLB as part of Post-TESL Certificate Training offered by TESL Ontario, to enhance current teacher development and professionalism, and to address the need for specialized training to meet evolving program and learner needs.

9. The CLB in the Employment Context

Recognizing the importance of language in an employment context has led to several CCLB initiatives. Since 2003, the CCLB has been involved in aligning the CLB with the Essential Skills Framework developed by the department then known as Human Resources and Skills Development Canada (HRSDC). Work-related skills, including some communication ones, are defined in Essential Skills profiles, which are used nationally to define the skills required to work in a wide range of occupations. The Essential Skills discuss communication in terms of native speakers of English, so that when they are aligned with the CLB they more adequately support second-language speakers. The 2005 *Comparative Framework* aligned CLB skills with four of the nine Essential Skills, although the document concedes that this is not a straightforward alignment, but rather an intersection that reflects the complex and multi-dimensional relationship between two very different underlying scales and constructs (CCLB 2005). Between 2000 and 2012, many occupations developed and/or put in place national standards for individuals working in an occupation or profession. In many occupations, there are also expectations that a second-language speaker must be able to work safely in the occupation/profession and that language ability plays a key role in almost all jobs.

The CCLB continues to work with regulators across Canada as they grapple with how to determine fair, rigorous, valid, and cost-effective ways of removing the barriers that prevent internationally educated professionals from working in their field and to ensure that Canada effectively uses the human capital available to it. The CCLB assists employers and regulatory bodies through two key initiatives: Benchmarking of an occupation and Occupational Language Analyses (OLA). Benchmarking is a rigorous process that uses primary and secondary sources to document the language demands of an occupation. Increasingly sought after by regulatory bodies, the process provides a benchmark for each of the four language skills that can be used for entry-to-practice or for full-working-capacity, as determined by the regulatory body. Occupational Language Analyses (OLA) determine the language demands of an occupation using validated secondary sources, such as National Occupation Standards, along with the Essential Skills profiles, or sector-specific standards. The CCLB has benchmarked or developed OLAs for over 140 occupations to date. In addition, it has benchmarked all the Red Seal trade examinations to ensure fairness, validity, reliability, and transparency in their use with all candidates. Experience has shown that each sector and profession deals with questions around appropriate levels and ways to evaluate proficiency in different ways, but with a lot of cross-pollination of ideas and methods.

To meet the needs of stakeholders who work with immigrants in pre-employment, counselling, and hiring and/or retaining immigrants, the CCLB has developed several tools and resources for counsellors, teachers in bridging programs, human-resources personnel, sector councils, and employers that are available on the CCLB website (www.language.ca). These tools and resources include, among others: *Prior Learning and Assessment Checklist* (CCLB 2007a); *Workplace Language Assessment* (CCLB 2009); *Workplace Language Assessment Pre-Screener* for use by counsellors (CCLB 2007b); *Work Ready* – a paper and online resource for employers and counsellors (CCLB 2007c); and *Can Do Statements for Employment* (CCLB 2016b) for use by employers, counsellors, and individuals; as well as the CLB Essential Skills website (www.itsessential.ca).

10. Future of the CLB

"By articulating standards for language proficiency, all stakeholders can now speak a common language and make informed decisions regarding settlement, training and employment opportunities" (Pawlikowska-Smith 2000). Formulated so confidently in the CLB 2000, these words implied that the CLB were firmly entrenched in Canada and integral to all components of settlement and language. As the national consultation on the CLB (which led to revised English and French versions of the standard in 2012) showed, this had not completely happened. The standard had continued to evolve and it continues to evolve to this day. It is a living document that supports the changing needs of immigration in Canada within a rigorous and reliable framework. In the early twenty-first century, an influx of immigrants with higher levels of English, the *Immigration and*

Refugee Protection Act (IRPA), and the need to meet the demands of employers led to the CLB being used in higher-stakes context. The CLB, under the stewardship of the CCLB, were flexible enough to respond to these changing demands. The revised 2012 standard brings the increased rigour and validity that will enable its use to support significant decisions around immigration and citizenship.

As has been shown in this chapter, there are many recent tools and resources to support the use of the CLB 2012 in Canada. The tools mentioned here are only the ones in which the CCLB played a development role.

Tool development, teacher training, and professional development need to be ongoing to support teachers and assessors. However, language training is often one of the first things cut during economic downturns, which in turn impacts training of instructors. It also impacts instructor skill sets, which, for publicly funded programs including the CLB and PBLA, are not yet covered in TESL training programs to any great degree.

The CCLB, as an organization that depends on project-based funding, is extremely vulnerable to economic downturns: its ability to support the community of practice is often severely limited. With funding cuts in many areas, it is even more critical to have an organization like the CCLB to provide the integrity, capacity, accountability, and reliability needed to deliver support for both the National Assessment System and LINC programs across Canada. To maintain the integrity of the standard, there must be stable investment in it.

Canada cannot be complacent about the CLB. Their reputation in Canada and internationally is growing, but they are as well under pressure from other standards that are making inroads into Canada. There are many questions about their future use, and also many possibilities. It is possible that, in the future, the use of the CLB will be expanded: for pre-arrival language and employment preparation, in a global language training context, and for entry into higher education in Canada. One barrier to expansion is that there is currently no CLB-referenced test used for these purposes, although the *Milestones* could possibly be used for such purposes in the future. With changes in government, there is no clear focus on the importance of the standard in an evolving economic and political environment. This includes clarification around the ongoing role of the CLB within the immigration process, and how language training supports all successful settlement and integration efforts for newcomers.

What is next for the CLB and the CCLB? In the next few years, concentrated efforts should be aimed at supporting the strategic growth of the standard and the organization that supports its implementation. The standard must be maintained and monitored for appropriate use to ensure its rigour and validity. Research is needed on the applicability of the CLB to immigrant youth aged 14 to 18, possible use with Canada's indigenous population, and their relevance internationally, so that their use may grow appropriately. Correlations with other standards and tests need to be conducted to provide consistent and reliable information to stakeholders and to ensure that the CLB are further nationally and internationally recognized, not just in the settlement language field but also in academic and workplace fields, as being valid, fair, and reliable for high-stakes purposes.

As the CLB attain their 20th anniversary in 2016, it is apparent that they have successfully evolved to meet current demands, but that they need nurturing to continue their growth in Canada and to meet future demands in Canada and internationally.

References

Bachman, Lyle F. 1990. *Fundamental Considerations in Language Testing*. Oxford: Oxford University Press.

Bachman, Lyle F., and Adrian Palmer. 1996. *Language Testing in Practice: Designing and Developing Useful Language Tests*. New York: Oxford University Press.

———. 2010. *Language Assessment Practice: Developing Language Assessments and Justifying Their Use in the Real World*. New York: Oxford University Press.

Blakely, Gregg, and Dipna Singh. 2012. "Federal and Provincial Policy Initiatives. LINC and CLIC: Looking back, looking forward." *INSCAN* Special Issue on Settlement Language Training: 7–11. Accessed March 10, 2016. http://www3.carleton.ca/cimss/inscan-e/v24_se.pdf.

Bournot-Trites, Monique, and Ross Barbour. 2012. Unpublished Report on Phases I and II of the Validation of the Canadian Language Benchmarks and Niveaux de Compétence Linguistique Canadiens. Ottawa: Centre for Canadian Language Benchmarks.

Bournot-Trites, Monique, Ross Barbour, Monika Jezak, Gail Stewart, and Daphné Blouin Carbonneau. 2015. *Theoretical Framework for the CLB and NCLC*. Ottawa: Centre for Canadian Language Benchmarks.

Celce-Murcia, Marianne, Zoltan Dörnyei, and Sarah Thurrell. 1995. "Communicative Competence: A Pedagogically Motivated Model with Content Specifications." *Issues in Applied Linguistics* 6(2): 5–35.

Centre for Canadian Language Benchmarks. 2004. *Summative Assessment Tasks for Canadian Language Benchmarks, Stage 1*. Ottawa: Centre for Canadian Language Benchmarks.

———. 2005. *Relating Canadian Language Benchmarks to Essential Skills: A Comparative Framework*. Ottawa: Centre for Canadian Language Benchmarks.

———. 2007a. *Prior learning and assessment checklist*. Ottawa: Centre for Canadian Language Benchmarks.

———. 2007b. *Workplace Language Assessment Pre-Screener*. Ottawa: Centre for Canadian Language Benchmarks. Accessed March 1, 2016. http://www.language.ca.

———. 2007c. *Work Ready*. Ottawa: Centre for Canadian Language Benchmarks. Accessed March 1, 2016. http://www.language.ca.

———. 2008. *CLB 5-10 Exit Tasks*. Ottawa: Centre for Canadian Language Benchmarks.

———. 2009. *Workplace Language Assessment Tool*. Ottawa: Centre for Canadian Language Benchmarks. Accessed March 1, 2016. http://www.language.ca.

———. 2012. *CLB Support Kit*. Ottawa: Centre for Canadian Language Benchmarks. Accessed March 1, 2016. http://www.language.ca.

———. 2013. *Trousse de soutien en français langue seconde*. Ottawa: Centre for Canadian Language Benchmarks. Accessed March 1, 2016. http://www.language.ca.

———. 2014. *Can Do Statements*. Ottawa: Centre for Canadian Language Benchmarks.

———. 2015. *Annual Report*. Ottawa: Centre for Canadian Language Benchmarks. Accessed March 1, 2016. http://www.language.ca.

———. 2016a. *The Canadian Language Benchmarks*. Accessed March 1, 2016. http://www.language.ca.

———. 2016b. *Can Do Statements for Employment*. Ottawa: Centre for Canadian Language Benchmarks. Accessed March 1, 2016. http://www.language.ca.

Citizenship and Immigration Canada. 2000. *Canadian Language Benchmarks 2000: ESL for Literacy Learners*. Ottawa: CIC and Government of Manitoba.

———. 2013. *National Language Placement and Progression Guidelines*. Ottawa: Citizenship and Immigration Canada.

Citizenship and Immigration Canada, and Centre for Canadian Language Benchmarks. 2012. *Canadian Language Benchmarks: English as a second*

language for adults. Ottawa: Citizenship and Immigration Canada. Accessed March 1, 2016. http://www.language.ca.
———. 2014. *Canadian Language Benchmarks: ESL for Adult Literacy Learners*. Ottawa: CIC. Accessed March 1, 2016. http://www.language.ca.
Cohen, Carolyn, and Antonella Valeo. 2012. *Enhancing Professionalism: A Framework for Post TESL Certificate Training, INSCAN* Special Issue on Settlement Language Training: 35–38. Accessed March 10, 2016. http://www3.carleton.ca/cimss/inscan-e/v24_se.pdf.
Council of Europe. 2001. *Common European Framework of Reference for Languages: Learning, Teaching, Assessment*. Strasbourg: Language Policy Unit.
Farrell, Thomas S. 2012. *Reflective Writing for Language Teachers*. Frameworks for Writing Series. Sheffield, UK: Equinox Publishing. Accessed on March 10, 2016. http://www.teslcanadajournal.ca/index.php/tesl/article/view/1170/990.
Holmes, Tara. 2005. *Integrating CLB assessment into your ESL classroom*. Ottawa: Centre for Canadian Language Benchmarks.
Makosky, Luke. 2008. *The Feasibility and Way Forward for a Standardized Exit Assessment and Test for Newcomers in LINC Training*. Ottawa: Citizenship and Immigration Canada.
Nagy, Philip, and Gail Stewart. 2009. *Research Study on Potential Approaches to Second Language Assessment*. Ottawa: Citizenship and Immigration Canada.
Norton Peirce, Bonny, and Gail Stewart. 1997. "The Development of Canadian Language Benchmarks Assessment." *TESL Canada Journal* 14(2): 17–31.
Pawlikowska-Smith, Grazyna. 2000. *Canadian Language Benchmarks 2000: English as a Second Langauge for Adults*. Ottawa: Centre for Canadian Language Benchmarks.
Pettis, Joanne. 2014. *Portfolio Based Language Assessment (PBLA): Guide for Teachers and Programs*. Ottawa: Centre for Canadian Language Benchmarks.
Rogers, Eleanor. 1993. "National working group on language benchmarks meets." *TESL Canada Bulletin*: 1.
Smit, Pamela, and Paul Turcot. 2010. *National Consultation on the Canadian Language Benchmarks 2000 and Niveaux de competence linguistique canadiens 2006: Final report*. Ottawa: Citizenship and Immigration Canada.

CHAPTER 5

The NCLC in Minority Settings: Past and Future Projects

Élissa Beaulieu
CCLB
Morgan Le Thiec
Université du Québec à Montréal, Consultant to CCLB

1. Introduction

In 2002, the Centre for Canadian Language Benchmarks (CCLB) set out to develop a French version of the *Canadian Language Benchmarks* (CLB) (CIC 1996). This "working document," *Standards linguistiques canadiens 2002* (CIC and CCLB 2002), was revised in 2006 and renamed *Niveaux de compétence linguistique canadiens 2006: français langue seconde pour adultes* (NCLC) (CIC and CCLB 2006). Last revised in 2012, the NCLC are a national standard for developing tools, resources, and training in French as a second language (FSL) in minority settings (CIC and CCLB 2012).

The goal of this chapter is to present several major initiatives based on the NCLC, designed for contexts where French is a minority language. First, we provide a brief overview of those particular contexts, and the specific needs this environment creates for stakeholders involved with FSL programs for adult immigrants. Next, we present a number of recent and ongoing projects divided into four categories: 1) immigrant placement and certification, 2) tools and resources for immigrants' language training, 3) support for instructors and other stakeholders involved with immigrant integration, and 4) FSL for the workplace. Following this project overview, we detail some of the challenges and opportunities identified by the CCLB French team and suggest some possible avenues for action in the years ahead.

2. Background

2.1 French as a minority language in Canada

Having two official languages in Canada means that in all regions English and French speakers shall have access to public services in the language of their choice. Section 34 of the *Official Languages Act* (Government of Canada 1988)[1] states that English and French are the languages of work in all federal institutions. Section 39 ensures equal opportunities for English-speaking and French-speaking Canadians for employment and advancement in federal institutions. Section 41 states that the government of Canada is committed to fostering the use of both English and French in Canadian society. Thus, services shall be provided to the public in a minority language where there is deemed to be a clear need. Those rules apply to Crown corporations and federal departments, to some provincial services offered according to provincial policies in force, and to educational services in elementary and secondary schools in regions where there is an acknowledged need, some of which are designated bilingual regions. In Ontario, for example, these include Ottawa, various towns in the county of Glengarry, Prescott, and Russell in the east, and the counties of Algoma, Sudbury, and Nipissing in the north.

However, official recognition of the French language and of Francophone language rights doesn't solve everything. In fact, access to services in French largely depends on having a sufficient concentration of French speakers living in a given area. And French is still very much a minority language in Canada: just over a million native French speakers reside outside of Quebec. Moreover, a certain number among this population no longer uses French in their daily lives. Furthermore, French-speaking minorities are spread across a vast territory in communities that vary widely in size from one region to another, and that in some cases are highly dispersed (Corbeil 2014).

This is the context in which language services are created and developed. Adult immigrants who wish to learn one of the two official languages within the framework of the CLB/NCLC must choose either English or French. They cannot do both. This fact affects registration on the French side because adult immigrants opt for programs that will help them integrate into Canadian society as quickly as possible. English, the majority language, is therefore largely favoured. The motivation to learn French must come from elsewhere:

- Participation in community life in a Francophone environment where, among other things, immigrants can register their children in French schools, study in French, and take advantage of available French-language services.
- Professional prospects associated with federal services that promote bilingualism.
- Professional environments where a strong command of French as a second official language is an asset or a path to promotion.
- A good understanding of the linguistic environment in which, unlike French, English can be learned outside the classroom because it is the dominant language of daily life.

For an FSL program for adult immigrants to succeed, many criteria must be met. First, language services must take into account the minority context in which the language is used, so they can offer realistic and rewarding learning opportunities. Second, those services must aim at a twofold objective—to enable adult immigrants to live and work in French if they so wish, and strengthen French-speaking minority communities by helping them integrate immigrants. We elaborate on those imperatives in the next section of this chapter.

2.2 Needs of FSL stakeholders

In 2007, the CCLB published the results of a study on how FSL stakeholders felt about the use of the NCLC 2006. The goal of this study, titled *Perceptions des intervenants en français langue seconde sur l'utilisation des NCLC 2006* (Dancose and Ricard 2007), was to explore how the NCLC 2006 performed with regard to two main functions of education standards, as identified by the German Ministry of Education and Research (2004):

- to provide stakeholders in charge of instruction (managers and teachers) with specific benchmarks to help guide their decisions and practices, based on a common language and a shared understanding of the learning progression.
- to provide a framework for assessing learner outcomes and giving constructive feedback, for both trainers and trainees.

In order to carry out the study, five focus groups were tasked with discussing the following points: intervention practices and programs, the needs of learners and stakeholders, the level of interest in adopting the NCLC, and steps for implementing the NCLC. The results allowed researchers to pinpoint the needs of FSL stakeholders and possible applications for the NCLC. They helped as well to identify the necessary steps for successfully implementing the NCLC framework.

Among others, this research highlighted the difficulty of transferring a learner from one institution to another because programs were not standardized. Furthermore, the lack of accurate assessment tools also prevented stakeholders from effectively measuring learners' progress, guiding them to appropriate training, or even assessing their FSL skills for purposes of employment. Lastly, the stakeholders showed a concern about determining which language-teaching model was most appropriate in an environment where French was a minority language.

In terms of possible NCLC applications, the participants of the study agreed on several points:

- **To use the NCLC as a national standard.** This would ensure that skill levels were comparable across all provinces. A learner trained in Manitoba who has achieved NCLC level 5 should be capable to perform the same language tasks as someone trained to the same NCLC level in New Brunswick. That way, language learners could move from one province to another and have their NCLC level recognized when joining a new language training program.
- **To standardize language training programs.** The standardization would make migration easier for a population that is often mobile in the first few years in Canada, and would also facilitate program evaluations and exchanges between stakeholders.
- **To meet the needs of adult learners.** The descriptors in the NCLC would allow learners to determine where they were on the learning continuum, based on clearly identified language tasks and communicative requirements anchored in real-life situations relevant to them.
- **To strengthen the link between NCLC-based language training and job search.** Reinforcing this link would help learners better meet the requirements for the occupation or profession they sought.

Several projects were developed in response to the 2007 study. At the present time, some of them are completed, while others are still underway. In general, they were designed to support FSL stakeholders (learners, instructors, program managers, vocational training providers, and others) by standardizing content and practices. The projects also dovetail with efforts by Immigration, Refugees and Citizenship Canada (IRCC) to meet quality assurance requirements in the educational field, which is a cornerstone of effective training (Harvey 2008, OCDE 2015).

The past and current projects (tests, language programs, instructor training, and tools specifically intended for workplace or other particular needs) that we will detail in the following section aim at benefiting all FSL stakeholders and at promoting integration.

3. NCLC-Related Projects

The grouping of the projects listed in this section highlights both their diversity and their common elements. We distinguish four categories of projects: 1) immigrant placement and certification, 2) tools and resources for language training for immigrants, 3) support for instructors and other stakeholders involved with immigrant integration, and 4) FSL for the workplace.

3.1 Immigrant placement and certification
Batterie de tests de classement (BTC-NCLC)
One of the means to standardize teaching is the development of placement and performance tests. The first of these tools, the BTC-NCLC, was created in 2009. It is a placement test that assesses a learner's language skills in four areas: writing, reading, speaking, and listening at NCLC levels 1 to 8. The test is used to place candidates in a language training program in an appropriate class. The BTC-NCLC was updated in 2015. The original test was three hours and fifteen minutes long. It satisfactorily assessed the language skills of the learner, but took too long to administer. At the request of IRCC, the CCLB created a shorter version of the test that also took into account the 2012 NCLC updates. This version was designed so as not to undermine the validity of the original test. Standardization efforts then continued with the creation of a high-stakes test that would legitimize completing an NCLC level.

Batterie de tests de rendement (BTR-NCLC)
In 2012, CIC (now IRCC) tasked the CCLB with creating a standardized FSL performance test. The BTR-NCLC was modelled on

the NCLC placement test (BTC), described in the previous section. Based on levels 3 to 9 of the NCLC, the test can be used in high-stakes situations (for official recognition of a skill level, certification, and so on).

The CCLB's task was to:

- Establish common components for the BTC-NCLC and the BTR-NCLC
- Ensure that these components matched the new 2012 standards
- Develop tasks meeting the requirements of a high-stakes test. For example, it was necessary to create enough equivalent tasks to have various versions of the test

Like the BTC-NCLC, the BTR assesses four language skills. Listening and reading are evaluated through multiple-choice questions associated with videos and written texts. The writing section is made up of four written tasks that progress from easy to difficult. Speaking is tested in a one-on-one interview that lasts roughly twelve minutes. The tasks become more and more difficult as the test progresses. Two equivalent versions of the test were created to ensure its usability. This way, a learner who has to retake the test will be presented with another version.

3.2 Tools and resources for immigrants' language training
CLIC en ligne
Immigrant learners more often than not lead demanding lives and must balance work, or work search, with family responsibilities. To study can be challenging. In French-speaking minority communities, particularly those located far from major urban centres, it is hence important to provide the learner with favourable learning conditions. Online training resources meet this goal.

The CLIC en ligne project (Cours de langue pour les immigrants au Canada) is an online immigrant language training initiative funded by the Ontario region of Citizenship and Immigration Canada (CIC), now IRCC. The project was initially developed by the Conseil des écoles publiques de l'est de l'Ontario, then by the CCLB. The Centre franco-ontarien de ressources pédagogiques was in charge of developing the online platform for the course. The CLIC en ligne is an asynchronous course. It has activities for listening, reading, and writing. Speaking skills are developed during online classes through weekly individual one-on-one sessions with an instructor. The activities reflect the requirements of NCLC levels 3 to 7 (Le Thiec 2013).

The learner is assigned ten themed units. The themes selected for the project were family, relationships and leisure activities, housing, travel and transportation, consumption, services, health, citizenship, education, employment, and Canada. These themes are relevant to all immigrants but have been adapted to meet the needs of FSL learners in minority settings. For instance, it was important to help students identify French-language immigrant-support services in Ontario.

To summarize, the CLIC en ligne project was required to cater to the specific needs of learners. The asynchronous training model was chosen to encourage learners to pursue their learning. Alternating between self-directed learning and interaction with an instructor has proven to be a successful and motivating format.

Portfolio-Based Language Assessment (PBLA)
In their technical reports to the CIC, Makosky (2008) and Nagy and Stewart (2009) drew attention to the fact that the assessment in the NCLC-related programs was neither systematic nor standardized. Those reports underscored the need for the federal government to implement a more authentic language-assessment protocol developed by instructors in federal language training programs. The project stemming out of these recommendations was the *Portfolio-Based Language Assessment* (PBLA).

PBLA is a collaborative approach that engages the instructor and the learner throughout the teaching/learning process. Together, they set language-learning goals, compile numerous examples of language performance and learning in a variety of contexts over time, analyse these examples, and review progress. The examples of completed language tasks show the learner's progress and areas for improvement. Compiling meaningful tasks during the learning process encourages FSL students to become more autonomous, active, and self-aware, and to take responsibility for their learning. The PBLA facilitates the acquisition of metacognitive strategies and skills that learners can put into practice in other learning contexts. The portfolio is a written document that defines, demonstrates, and compiles an individual's learning outcomes with respect to an objective (Legendre 2005, 1059).

The portfolio presents itself as a binder given to each new student to support their language learning and facilitate their settlement in Canada. The binder for French students is called *Mon Portfolio NCLC*. It was translated and adapted from the English binder, *The Language Companion*. There are three versions of *Mon Portfolio NCLC*: FSL literacy, NCLC 1–4, and NCLC 5–8. The language level for each version of the portfolio is adjusted according to the language abilities of each category of learners (literacy, beginner, intermediate).

Portfolios may be used for diverse purposes and to meet various objectives (Scallon 2004). *Mon Portfolio NCLC* is used as an assessment tool and for learning. Portfolios may also be used to help each student become aware of their learning, to maintain the focus on what they have already mastered and what they still have to learn, to develop strategies to fill in the learning gaps, and to set learning goals (Scallon 2004, 305). In addition to supporting the learners as they use their portfolios, instructors can also use the portfolio to review their teaching methods: Are they effective, or are new strategies needed to help students progress further?

In a minority environment, the portfolio is a particularly valuable tool, because it helps the learner find language resources for living in French. It is the link between the learners' needs, their personal language learning, and the French-speaking community they would like to get to know. The portfolio includes a list of websites for Francophone community organizations in each Canadian province where adults are taught with the NCLC. It also contains space for the learner to add information about their province's geography, government, transportation options, and more.

Literacy levels
Certain adult immigrants who wish to take FSL classes may, for various reasons, need to develop their literacy skills as well. Some of them may come from oral cultures or from places that do not use the Roman alphabet, while others may have had little or no schooling before their arrival in Canada.

Regular FSL classes do not meet the particular needs of this population, so specific courses need to be created. Using the CLB document *ESL for Adult Literacy Learners* (CIC and CCLB 2014a) as a reference, the CCLB French team undertook the development of an FSL literacy document that accounts for the Francophone minority context (CIC and CCLB 2014b).

3.3 Support for language instructors and other stakeholders in immigrant integration

Portfolio-Based Language Assessment (PBLA) training
To train instructors to use the PBLA is a vital step in implementing the portfolio and ensuring standardized practices. To this end, an online training tool was designed and delivered using a train-the-trainer model. The first users of the tool were instructors designated as *champions* of PBLA. They were selected on the basis of their previous training and experience. These *champion* instructors received twenty hours of distance training. Once the course completed, they became a resource and the instructors for their co-workers. In sum, PBLA training relies on teamwork and revolves around projects, readings, and themed discussions.

PBLA training does more than prepare instructors to use the portfolio. It also builds the capacity of teachers so they can work independently and meet the requirements for standardized language services and reporting. To meet this goal, the training involves a review of more general educational concepts and provides useful guidelines for teaching with the NCLC, such as principles for needs analysis or for task-based assessment. Since portfolio use is mandatory in NCLC-related programs, it is important as well to provide instructors with the resources necessary to understand its usefulness and challenges.

One of the major goals of PBLA training is to raise teachers' awareness of the particularity of minority contexts and of the importance to cater to the specific learners' language needs. As an assessment tool, the PBLA does not set out a series of specific tasks, but rather focuses on principles that encourage instructors to create tasks similar to those that learners will perform in their daily lives. Indeed, some language tasks are not relevant in French minority contexts; for instance, grocery shopping, job search, or many other commercial services. The important thing, as with any NCLC tool, is than to adapt the teaching content to meet the learners' needs, depending on the French-language situation in their particular community.

Curriculum Guidelines for the Ontario
Non-Credit Adult Language Training Program
The Curriculum Guidelines for the Ontario Non-Credit Adult Language Training Program project was funded in 2014 by the Ontario

Ministry of Citizenship, Immigration and International Trade (MCIIT). The project has been developed as an interactive portal that includes:

- A report on the founding principles of non-credit adult language training
- An online planning tool in both official languages intended for ESL and FSL stakeholders

The online planning tool is called *Quartz* in reference to Ontario's official mineral, amethyst. The project was created by two teams, each representing one of the official languages: the Centre for Canadian Language Benchmarks and the Toronto Catholic District School Board. Drawing from the NCLC and CLB, studies and surveys on ESL/FSL teaching in Canada and worldwide, and the situation of French and English in Ontario, the two teams prepared a document that listed eight founding principles for FSL:

- Principle 1: FSL programs are focused on the learner
- Principle 2: FSL programs are developed according to specific stakeholders' needs
- Principle 3: FSL programs apply the principles of the communicative approach
- Principle 4: The learning objectives are explicit
- Principle 5: Assessment is used to verify that learning objectives are reached and to provide course information
- Principle 6: Teaching FSL relies on recognized and shared skills
- Principle 7: Managing FSL programs facilitates course access and guidance for learners
- Principle 8: FSL programs are accountable to the community

Quartz was designed to make it easier to apply these principles and standardize practices. It supports course planning, from the most general information (course title, skills covered, course schedule, and so on) to the most specific (language content targeted, teaching sequence, and so on). It helps instructors plan the teaching and the assessment.

This tool offers a traditional three-level course structure: course, unit, and lesson. A course is made up of a series of units, each consisting of a group of lessons. An instructor may plan a course, unit, or lesson, and all those planning levels are interlinked.

This means that information selected on the course level is maintained throughout the planning process and allows data to be filtered. The interactive planning allows teachers and program administrators to choose content proposed in *Quartz* or add their own information, such as:

- Course, unit, and lesson titles
- Needs (things learners do as part of their daily lives)
- Themes and subthemes
- Real-life tasks (communicative tasks that learners accomplish as part of their daily lives)
- Skills that need to be developed in order to accomplish real-life tasks
- Language content (grammar, vocabulary, and so on)
- Skill-building activities, e.g., traditional activities that target a particular aspect of language related to real life tasks
- Assessment activities that allow learners to demonstrate their ability to complete a task in authentic settings (users can choose or create an assessment format that suits their needs)

The planning tool generates a document that can be printed as well as saved. It compiles all the selected or added information.

Quartz also offers a catalogue of resources, so instructors can read about various topics (needs analysis, task-based teaching, task-based assessment, and more) or use documents made available to them for teaching, including samples of needs analysis forms, assessment forms, or even complete units.

FSL instructors who use the NCLC, unlike those on the English side, do not currently have the benefit of accredited training, which is a big drawback of the NCLC-related programs, since such training is vital to professionalize the instructor's role and to standardize teaching and assessment practices. Although it cannot compensate for this gap, *Quartz* does provide a training framework, as well as many resources and application examples that account for the particularities of FSL teaching in minority settings. For example, a resource database was created with authentic tasks in French minority contexts. These tasks are categorized according to relevant topics and the needs of the FSL learners integrating into their French-speaking community, such as:

- understanding the history of French-speaking minorities and participating in Francophone cultural life
- understanding language rights and defending the right to live in French
- knowing and using services in French

Those themes were completed with a list of resources for French-speaking minorities in Canada, including media, French-language services, and online historical resources.

To conclude, the main contribution of *Quartz* lies in the fact that it supports standardizing practices in the NCLC teaching community, where instructors sometimes work far from large urban centres and their attendant pedagogical resources, and where teacher training can vary widely from one instructor to another.

Training workshops for instructors
In addition to training based on the PBLA and the Curriculum Guidelines for the Ontario Non-Credit Adult Language Training Program project, instructors also receive classroom training on various subjects, such as the NCLC, task-based teaching, or assessments using the NCLC.

The combination of these different training methods favours a long-term learning process aimed at strengthening the FSL community of practice. It gives both new and experienced instructors, as well as program managers, considerable flexibility in terms of their professional development. It makes it possible to train the stakeholders rapidly, and facilitates regular review of the guidelines for NCLC-based teaching.

3.4 FSL for the workplace
Workplace Language Assessment (WLA) pre-screening tool
Many professions in Canada require a language proficiency level of NCLC 6, 7, or even 8. Bridge-to-work programs expect immigrants who have studied French outside Canada to have a minimum NCLC level 6 if they are to fully benefit from those programs. To this end, the CCLB developed a tool to assess whether or not an internationally educated person has attained a minimum of a NCLC level 6.

The WLA is a pre-screening tool, not a language test. It helps instructors advise and guide immigrants educated outside of Canada who aim at preparing for postsecondary entrance exams, pursuing postsecondary studies, taking part in bridge-to-work programs, finding a job, or passing a language test.

The WLA was first created in 2007 for English speakers. An adapted version was developed in 2015 for FSL. It evaluates candidates' reading, writing, listening, and speaking skills. As part of the test, the internationally educated person fills out a form, which includes a reading and writing activity. Then they have an interview with a counsellor. The test is simple and quick: it takes about thirty minutes to complete. The content was developed to meet the requirements for the NCLC 6 level.

In addition to the language ability assessment, the WLA was created to help new immigrants understand Canadian workplace language requirements, which vary depending on the occupation.

Training for WLA is available online so that all job counsellors can access it, whether they are in urban centres or in remote areas.

Can Do *checklists*

In 2013, at the request of MCIIT, the *Can Do* checklists (based on the twelve benchmarks and four skills) were updated. The checklists are intended for learners and instructors alike. They describe learners' performance, level by level, in clear, simple language. For instance, for reading, the learner may be able to "compare information in one or more texts." An example of this skill would be: "I can read a simple description of two elementary schools and decide where I should register my child."

In 2015, based on these lists, the *Can Do for Workplace*, aiming at NCLC levels 4 to 10, were developed and adapted for three different groups: immigrants, employers, and employment counsellors. The checklists provide insight – from the point of view of the immigrant, the employer, and the job counsellor – into what an immigrant is capable to do employment-wise in terms of his or her language skills. Immigrants can use these lists to get a better idea of what they can and can't do in terms of the language requirements of the job they seek. Employers can use the lists to assess the language requirements of the job and the NCLC level required to fill it. Employment counsellors can better advise immigrants by making a link between their NCLC current level and their professional goals.

4. Conclusion: Challenges and Opportunities of FSL Teaching in Minority Settings

Standardizing official-language teaching and assessment for adult immigrants in Canada, as well as quality assurance in this domain, are long-term undertakings. Since the first version of the French benchmarks in 2002, an impressive amount of work has been accomplished toward those goals: the standard was revised twice, and a common theoretical framework was developed for both French and English. In the same vein, a large array of tools and resources were recently proposed for learners, teachers, and other FSL stakeholders. Some of them are detailed in this chapter and others can be found on the dedicated website: www.language.ca. In conclusion, we would like to outline some major challenges and opportunities for FSL adult immigrant training in Canada, as perceived by the CCLB French team. Our discussion revolves around four themes: 1) improving access to information and French-language resources, 2) developing content adapted to the French minorities' settings, 3) seeking adequate FSL teacher training, and 4) building a coherent community of practice.

First, according to a 2012 Office of the Commissioner of Official Languages report, bilingual resources are extensive, but often hard to access. French-language resources and services clearly face visibility challenges in a minority context dominated by English. That is why it is important to compile and categorize them on regular basis and pass this information on to the instructors, so they can use it effectively in their classrooms. Some of this work was done recently through tools such as the PBLA or the *Trousse de soutien en Français langue seconde* (CCLB 2013), but this line of work must continue, since this information and resources quickly become outdated.

Second, it is essential to create content adapted to the minority contexts, where French is not used in all aspects of daily life. It is important to remain pragmatic and realistic about language use in order to provide real-life solutions for instructors and learners. To propose truly authentic language tasks is an ongoing struggle while developing tools for those teaching, learning, and assessment environments.

Third, to standardize teaching methodology in French as a minority language classrooms remains challenging. Teacher training is the cornerstone of a unified vision of instruction. For example, instructors in the CLB network receive accredited training, which helps a lot in standardizing teacher practices. The NCLC network has no equivalent program. FSL instructors receive extensive training, but there is no official certification. Such accreditation could potentially increase teacher retention rates for this highly fluctuating workforce.

Finally, the CLB community of practice is well known across Canada as having a distinctive "Benchmarks culture." The NCLC practitioners struggle to create such a community. Many factors contribute to this situation: lack of official accreditation, high turnover rate, small numbers of instructors and teaching institutions as compared to the CLB network, as well as their dispersal throughout Canada. This situation urgently calls for action. Accredited training would certainly foster a stronger dynamic in favour of standardization and quality assurance. At the very least, a competency profile for FSL instructors should be drawn up. Such a profile would help funding agencies manage training needs and provide training program managers with hiring guidelines. It would also help instructors plan their professional development. A learning portfolio based on the competency profile would enable instructors to set clear professional-development goals and develop the kind of reflective approach to their practice widely advocated since Schön's work (1983), and which they could share on occasion with their NCLC work team or trainers. Creating virtual and in-classroom professional learning communities (PLC) could be an interesting path to follow from a reflective practitioner perspective. A PLC is defined as a group of teachers who meet to examine in depth the processes of learning and teaching in order to improve their professional practices (Kristmanson et al. 2008, 43). Given the small number of instructors, it would surely be feasible to create links of this kind between institutions and provinces. PLC could help instructors improve their practice by sharing ideas and working collaboratively, and it would also promote a Francophone community of practice for NCLC nationwide. The community of practice would serve the interests of FSL instructors working with adult immigrants, and strengthen their status and role in maintaining and developing the Canadian Francophonie.

In conclusion of this chapter it is important to underline that these various tools and resources have been created to standardize practices across Canada. We must continue in this direction, but also work on more visibility for the French scale and on the recognition of its contribution to the Francophone minorities. In the years to come, it will also be important to create projects that will allow us to better characterize the teaching of French in a minority settings. A study of communication tasks in authentic French-minority contexts is a priority. We see the twentieth anniversary of the Centre for Canadian Language Benchmarks as an occasion to bring forward a positive outlook on the work accomplished and to look with ambition into the future.

References

Centre for Canadian Language Benchmarks. 2013. *NCLC: Trousse de soutien.* Ottawa: Centre for Canadian Language Benchmarks.
Citizenship and Immigration Canada. 1996. *Canadian Language Benchmarks: English as a Second Language for Adults. English as a second language for literacy learners (working document, 1996).* Ottawa: Minister of Supply and Services Canada.
Citizenship and Immigration Canada, and Centre for Canadian Language Benchmarks. 2002. *Standards linguistiques canadiens 2002: français langue seconde pour adultes.* Ottawa: Minister of Public Works and Services Canada.
———. 2006. *Niveaux de compétence linguistique canadiens 2006: français langue seconde pour adultes.* Ottawa: Citizenship and Immigration Canada.
———. 2012. *Niveaux de compétence linguistique canadiens français langue seconde pour adultes.* Ottawa: Citizenship and Immigration Canada.
———. 2014a. *Canadian Language Benchmarks: ESL for Adult Literacy Learners.* Ottawa: CIC.
———. 2014b. *Alphabétisation pour immigrants adultes en français langue seconde (FLS).* Ottawa: Centre for Canadian Language Benchmarks.
Corbeil, Jean-Pierre. 2014. *Document de travail sur la définition statistique de la population de langue française au Canada.* Presented at the Fédération des communautés francophones et acadiennes (FCFA) du Canada.
Dancose, Sylvia, and Philippe Ricard. 2007. *Perceptions des intervenants en français langue seconde sur l'utilisation des Niveaux de compétence linguistique canadiens 2006. Français langue seconde pour adultes dans leur contexte et milieu de travail.* Ottawa: Centre for Canadian Language Benchmarks.
Government of Canada. 1988. *Official Languages Act.* Accessed May 30, 2016. http://www.thecanadianencyclopedia.ca/en/article/official-languages-act-1988/.
Harvey, Lee. 2008. *Les initiatives canadiennes d'assurance de la qualité vues dans le contexte international.* Toronto: Council of Ministers of Education (CMEC). Accessed March 24, 2016. http://cmec.ca/Publications/Lists/Publications/Attachments/117/2008-05-lee-harvey.fr.pdf

Kristmanson, Paula, Joe Dicks, Josée Le Bouthillier, and Renée Bourgouin. 2008. "L'écriture en immersion française : Les meilleures pratiques et le rôle d'une communauté professionnelle d'apprentissage." *Revue canadienne de linguistique appliquée* 11(1) : 41–61.

Le Thiec, Morgan. 2013. "Le CLIC en ligne : enjeux et réponses." *Les Cahiers de l'ILOB* 5: 185–194.

Legendre, Robert. 2005. *Dictionnaire actuel de l'éducation*. Montreal: Éditions Guérin.

Makosky, Lyle. 2008. *The Feasibility and Way Forward for a Standardized Exit Assessment and Test for Newcomers in LINC Training*. Ottawa: Citizenship and Immigration Canada.

Ministry of Education and Research. 2004. *Le développement de standards nationaux de formation*. Bonn: Ministry of Education and Research. Accessed March 24, 2016. http://www.edudoc.ch/static/web/arbeiten/harmos/develop_standards_nat_form_f.pdf.

Nagy, Phil, and Gail Stewart. 2009. *Research Study on Potential Approaches to Second Language Assessment*. Ottawa: Citizenship and Immigration Canada.

Office of the Commissioner of Official Languages. 2012. *Rapport annuel du Commissariat aux langues officielles 2011–2012*. Ottawa: Commissariat aux langues officielles. Accessed March 24, 2016. http://www.ocol-clo.gc.ca/sites/default/files/ar_ra_2011_12_f.pdf.

Organisation for Economic Cooperation and Development. 2015. *Perspectives des politiques de l'Éducation 2015, des réformes en marche*. Paris: OECD.

Scallon, Gerard. 2004. *L'évaluation des apprentissages dans une approche par compétences*. Montreal: Éditions ERPI.

Schön, Donald A. 1983. *The Reflective Practitioner*. New York: Basic Books.

Note

[1] Complete information on the *Official Languages Act* is available on the Office of the Commissioner of Official Languages website: http://www.ocol-clo.gc.ca/fr/droits_linguistiques/act.

CHAPTER 6

Conclusion: Building a Bridge to the Future – Potential Contribution of the CLB and the NCLC

Samira ElAtia
University of Alberta, Campus Saint-Jean

In January 2005, I joined the English Language Program (ELP) at the University of Alberta as a research fellow working on language tests. Dr. Grazyna Pawlikowska-Smith had retired as the director of the ELP, so I never had the chance to meet her. However, I had the chance to get to know her fantastic work at the English Language Program, and of course her tremendous contribution to the original *Canadian Language Benchmarks* (CLB) – the 2000 edition (Pawlikowska-Smith 2000).

Prior to joining the University of Alberta and the ELP, I worked mainly with the guidelines of the American Council for the Teaching of Foreign Languages (ACTFL). As a language teacher, I received my training from Alice Omaggio-Hadley, who was a past president of ACTFL, and was well known for her work in language program development and language teaching around the ACTFL guidelines (Omaggio-Hadley 1993, 2001). In the summer of 2001, I even attended the examiner's training workshop for the ACTFL Oral Proficiency Interviews. During this time, the CLB were not well known beyond certain groups in Canada, let alone abroad.

As I worked with the CLB at ELP from 2005 on, I became more and more aware of their empirical value, of their clearly stated descriptors, and more important, of the fluidity of the materials developed to assist in their implementation. I appreciated their value for language program development: the CLB are straightforward, clear, precise, and among the very first language descriptors to use the *Can Do Statements* from a learner's perspective as part of their breaking down of the language competence components and constructs targeted at each level. It was during my tenure as the chair of the Task Force on Language Standards for the International Language Testing Association from 2007 to 2009 that I studied the CLB in depth. I did several critical comparative analyses of the ACTFL and the Common European Framework of Reference for Languages (CEFR) scales. To me, the CLB are pioneers, for they are specific to adult language competence within the Canadian context.

By 2008, when I attended the annual gathering of the International Language Testing Association, Language Testing Research Colloquium (LTRC) in China, several Canadian colleagues were presenting their assessment work anchored in the CLB, with a focus on language training and assessment for nursing, the CELBAN (namely the work of David Watt at the University of Calgary; see Watt and Lake 2000). With a strong contingent of Canadian specialists in language assessment, and with the CLB as a reference to use in assessment, we held our first meeting at that time to start formal talks about establishing a Canadian Association for Language Assessment.[1] At this time, the CLB had an international and national presence, with several academics and researchers using the CLB as framework for their work.

Last year, when I presented at the International Conference on Language Learning and Culture in Fairfax, Virginia (ElAtia 2015), I was surprised by how many American and overseas academics were familiar with the Benchmarks,[2] were speaking highly of them, and were referring to them for their research and program development. They were impressed by the updated edition of the CLB, as well as the uniquely developed Niveaux de compétence linguistique canadiens (NCLC).

Indeed, when in 2009 the Centre for Canadian Language Benchmarks (CCLB) decided to update the NCLC, they formed a team of specialists who spoke French, worked in French, and were aware of the French situation and nuances in Canada. They selected specialists who were knowledgeable of the legal and judicial situation of French, as well as the historical and political implications and realities of French in minority situations, in French immersion programs, and in bilingual contexts, as well as in unilingual Francophone contexts. The adaptation process that the NCLC underwent is a testament to how developing language programs in two languages should be done. Instead of going for a translation of the English CLB to French, the

NCLC were adapted and developed separately. French and English are two different languages that require different ways of teaching because of their nature, their cultural place in Canadian history, and their uses and mandates in Canada. The International Testing Commission (2011), in its twenty-two guidelines, emphasized the importance of the adaptation, and warned about the cultural and pragmatic components of a language that are not taken into consideration when translating (ElAtia 2011).

1. The CCLB and the Benchmarks: Vision, Mission, and Mandate for Language Acquisition

The CCLB is a national not-for-profit organization established in 1998, funded by the Canadian government, and "governed by a nationally representative, multi-stakeholder board of directors, including representation from government, ESL and FSL experts, and language assessors" (CCLB website 2016: www.language.ca).

The vision and mission statements of the Centre are stated as follows:

Vision
The Canadian Language Benchmarks and the Niveaux de compétence linguistique canadiens are the national standards recognized in Canada and internationally for describing, measuring and recognizing English and French language proficiency of immigrants and prospective immigrants destined for Canada.
Mission
The Centre for Canadian Language Benchmarks/Centre des niveaux de compétence linguistique canadiens leads and provides expertise in the implementation and dissemination of the Canadian Language Benchmarks and the Niveaux de compétence linguistique canadiens as practical, fair and reliable national standards of English and French language proficiency, in educational, training, community and workplace settings. (CCLB website 2016)

In the statement above, the last sentence articulates very clearly the scope of the Benchmarks. In line with this mission statement, the Centre strongly warns against the use of the Benchmarks outside of their intended context without valid research backing up such use.

However, since the Benchmarks have been developed by world-renowned specialists through a rigorous process, with a focus on adult language learners, the CCLB has the necessary expertise to offer guidelines and directives to all individuals and institutions in and outside of Canada that would like to use the Benchmarks as a reference.

2. Uniqueness of the Benchmarks as Descriptors

Performance descriptors (or guidelines) are statements of expected ability and/or competence in a language (ElAtia 2011). As such, the Benchmarks:

1. Serve as guidelines for curriculum design in language teaching, as scales for establishing item difficulty and establishing language constructs, and as criteria to be achieved at different levels of both teaching and assessment, and they serve as the genesis of language test tasks and items.
2. Serve in determining a person's proficiency in a language independent of any language learning program. These include a person who is not learning the language at the moment, or has not learned the language in a conventional academic way, but would like to know his or her proficiency level. Performance descriptors are not exclusively for educational needs, as they serve many other purposes, such as work, immigration, promotion, and/or personal interest (in knowing one's competence level in a language).
3. Serve test developers as language performance descriptors – test developers may refer to descriptors when constructing tests and when analyzing and making inferences about results.[3]

In short, the Benchmarks provide "a national framework of reference for the development of language learning programs, curricula and materials relevant to the needs of adult newcomers to Canada during the process of settlement and integration" (CCLB website 2016) for both official languages, French and English. They are used for "describing, measuring and recognizing the second language proficiency of adult immigrants and prospective immigrants for living and working in Canada" (CCLB website 2016).

The Benchmarks are composed of twelve levels divided into three proficiency stages – basic, intermediate, and advanced – covering the four classic language skills: listening, speaking, reading, and writing (see Table 6.1 below). In this regard, they are on a par with other state-of-the-art competency descriptors (see ElAtia 2011 for comparison between the CLB, the ACTFL, and the CEFR).

Table 6.1. Breakdown of Stages and Levels in CLB

Stage I	Stage II	Stage III
Basic proficiency **Benchmarks 1 to 4**	*Intermediate proficiency* **Benchmarks 5 to 8**	*Advanced proficiency* **Benchmarks 9 to 12**

The Benchmarks are context-specific. They serve distinct purposes in Canadian society, where French and English are the two official languages within a multicultural setting that allows all Canadians to maintain their cultures and their own native languages, be they Urdu, German, Mandarin, Cree, or any another language.

Among other researchers, Saville (2009, 26) stresses the need for "understanding test *purposes* and related *contexts*"; otherwise, several issues would arise from clashes between policy and decision makers on the one hand, and testing practitioners and examinees on the other hand. Hence, in a situation where a language test would be chosen by Canadian immigration officials to assess the language competence of adult immigrants, the Benchmarks should logically be selected as a point of reference for this test. If decision makers favour another set of competence descriptors, such as, for instance, the CEFR, and use a test that is calibrated using those levels, unfairness and validity threaten to hang over the decision-making process. Strong arguments need to be made to justify such a choice, since the Benchmarks already exist, developed in Canada, by a Canadian agency, to serve this very purpose of assessment. It would be questionable to use anything else that does not address the mandate and context of the particular Canadian testing situation. As an example of this good practice, in England and in the Netherlands, when officials were deciding on language assessment tools for immigration and citizenship purposes, the CEFR was selected without hesitation for establishing the appropriate level of competence, since both countries adhere to the Convention of Europe that mandates the use of the CEFR as a way to standardize language competence descriptors across Europe (Blackledge 2009, De Jong et al. 2009).

3. The Benchmarks, the CCLB, and Research

Because of their broad scope, the Benchmarks can play a major role in advancing research on language learning, language assessment, and language program development. In my opinion, the national and international future of both the Benchmarks and the CCLB lies in research. Indeed, for the first almost twenty years, the CCLB solidified its place within Canada as a leading agency for language program development and language learning and assessment. The coming years should be focused on branching out from the traditional portfolio and touching other populations and contexts where it can have an important impact. This will only materialize if solid diverse research is conducted on the Benchmarks. For this to happen, the CCLB would have to play a pivotal role. In the following sections of this paper, I elaborate on the chart below to outline the various contexts and potential research subjects connected with the Benchmarks, besides the clientele intended for the present time, that is, foreigners coming to work in Canada and adult immigrants settling in Canada.

Figure 6.1. CCLB and the Benchmarks: various potential areas of research

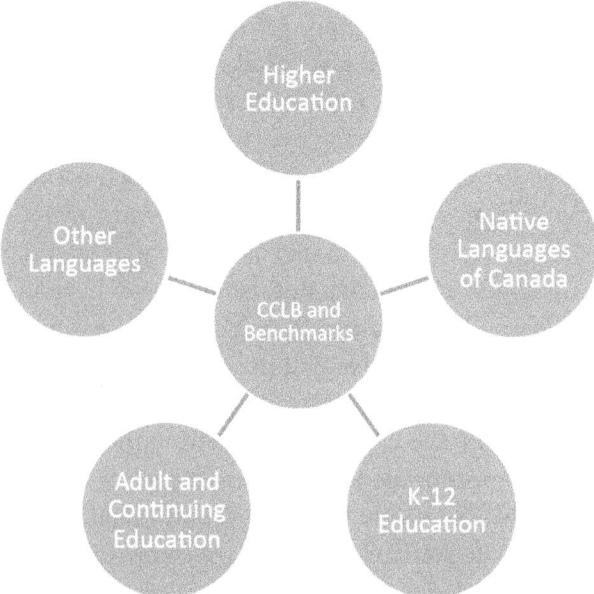

4. Higher Education: The First Frontier for the Benchmarks Research

In higher education, the use of the Benchmarks has become an urgent issue. There are three groups that could benefit greatly from research on the Canadian framework: international students, registrar offices, and language program developers.

International students

According to Saif (2013), international students make up a large and growing category. The majority of these students already fulfil, to some degree, the language requirements of their respective institutions. Others come to Canadian post-secondary institutions exclusively to learn English (or French), or to learn English (or French) as a prerequisite to another, more specialized or content-oriented, degree. In both these cases, the students are young adults who have completed grade 12, and hence the use of the Benchmarks would apply to them. Moreover, as mentioned earlier and demonstrated in various chapters of this book, the Benchmarks match other competency descriptors at the content level, they are meant for adult language education, and they target second-language speakers. Finally, they have been developed by Canadian experts for Canadian education and contexts. And yet, in higher-education language programs, in language progress assessment, and in admission criteria for language competence, they are not used.

Registrar offices

The Benchmarks would offer registrar officers and language program administrators a springboard to work from for placement, as well as for their program development and specification. They offer a solid platform of support to all those who use the related materials for assessment (diagnostic and placement), as well as for formative assessment, achievement, and most important, for competency assessment. The *Milestones* high-stakes test, described in chapter 3 of this book, holds great promise for language assessment in Canada. Research on the *Milestones*, as well as other batteries of assessments and tests developed by the CCLB, needs to be instigated from a variety of angles: course requirements, backwash, and content/construct validity – all within the framework of higher-education contexts. For this reason, the *Milestones* scores should also be considered as a Canadian alternative to the IELTS, TOEFL, CAEL, or other test scores that provide a snapshot about potential students' language proficiency.

Language program developers

The resources developed by the CCLB, described in chapters 3 and 4 of this book, offer a great support to the teachers and to language program developers. For instance, the materials developed for CELBAN, described in the chapter 4, demonstrate an excellent application to the Canadian context. Using this resource, one can therefore attest that students are able to function and to work in a Canadian reality once they finish their degrees. And yet again, such materials have been shunned by post-secondary institutions, except for some small programs. As a case in point, in my home institution, the University of Alberta, the ELP, the TESL, and the Faculty of Nursing are the only ones fully versed in and fully aware of the Benchmarks and the materials that the CCLB offers to supplement them.

Conclusion

Research on the applications of the Benchmarks in academic contexts is still lacking, and for their range of uses to improve, much work needs to be done. However, for this research to occur, and especially in order to determine funding, there needs to be a willingness on the part of the various stakeholders, both federally and provincially: the institutions of higher education and the provincial ministries of higher education, as well as various institutions of the federal government. For initial steps, Immigration, Refugees and Citizenship Canada (IRCC) may be very helpful, since international students have undergone the process for their visa and temporary residency status before joining their universities. Among the topics that need researching in the academic context are the following:

1. Language training for international students who are at the graduate level or working as teaching or research assistants. These students account for a large portion of the international students in Canada. Some of them, those who come in as immigrants or skilled workers, do receive thorough training via programs that are Benchmarks-based, but the rest do not. This needs to be studied

to establish the feasibility, validity, and accountability of such programs.
2. While the CLB are well anchored, the NCLC are much less so. As the fourth chapter of this book shows, the diverse, varied, and complex situations for Francophone education and French as a minority language programs for adults are much more precarious and need more investment. So far, Canadian institutions of higher education seek the tools and resources coming out of France to evaluate students and to develop programs. Moreover, they use indicators, books, materials, and tests developed in the United States. AlHamid and ElAtias's (2016) study regarding the stereotypes that students form concerning the variations of French in Western Canada is alarming: a majority of students who studied in French viewed the Metropolitan variety from France as superior to the Canadian one (Laurentian) because most of the materials come from France. Since the realities for French programs in Canadian higher education are very particular, they need to be studied within a unique cultural lens, such as the one proposed in the NCLC and related materials.
3. French immersion and Francophone stream programs should look closely at the products that accompany the NCLC (for instance, the self-assessment tools and the language portfolio assessment) for local solutions to local challenges. In fact, at the present date, assumptions about the level of language competence among students in these programs are diverse and sometimes contradictory, which poses challenges to admissions officers. Articulation committees in both British Columbia and Alberta, as well as the Language Consortia, are currently involved in intense discussions about the level of language competency in both French and English for students who finish high school and who register for university.

5. Continuing and Adult Education

If there is one place where the CLB has blossomed, it has been in the field of adult education. Within Employment and Social Development Canada (ESDC), formerly Human Resources Canada, there are at least two categories where the Benchmarks should be recognized and used: foreign workers and literacy/essential-skills development. In both, research is needed for implementation, for feasibility of validity, and fairness.

Foreign workers

Within the requirements of many jobs in Canada, the parameters for language proficiency are set for foreign workers. When establishing scores/setting standards for the specific jobs that target foreign workers, the common practice has been to refer to the guidelines established by IRCC. However, ESDC (2016) also states provisions for language that affect foreign workers, such as:

Language restriction provision
A distinct language assessment provision has been introduced as subsection 203 (1.01) of the Immigration and Refugee Protection Regulations. As a result, English and French are the only languages that can be identified as a job requirement both in job applications and in job advertisements by employers, unless they can demonstrate that another language is essential for the job.

Language proficiency provision for caregivers
Employers must ensure that the caregiver being hired speaks, reads, and understands at least one of Canada's official languages (English or French). Caregivers must have a level of fluency that enables them to communicate effectively and independently in an unsupervised setting.

When setting up the parameters for language requirements, some organizations do already refer to the CLB as indicators of language proficiency (see chapter 4 for more details), but much research still needs to be done with regard to setting standards for specific jobs – research that would include various stakeholders from hiring agencies, governing bodies, and associations of certain jobs and trades, as well as representatives from the CCLB. These stakeholders would make better-informed decisions that are fair and valid. In addition, research needs to be conducted for diagnostic and formative assessment after the foreign workers start their work, in order to longitudinally study the development of official-language skills among this group.

Essential skills and literacy

Among the major work that ESDC oversees is the literacy and essential-skills portfolio. According to ESDC, literacy and essential skills are needed for work, learning, and life; are the foundation for learning all other skills; and help people evolve with their jobs and adapt to workplace change.

Essential skills, and more particularly literacy, are of interest to many stakeholders across Canada. They are important indicators of the well-being of the active population in Canada, and can be revealing about the state of education, as well as the economic and social status of Canadians (including rates of poverty and crime). Essential skills:

> include the skills associated with literacy (i.e. reading, writing, document use and numeracy) but go beyond to also include thinking skills, oral communication, computer use/digital skills, working with others and the skills associated with continuous learning. They provide the foundation for learning all other skills and enable people to better prepare for, get and keep a job, and adapt and succeed at work. (ESDC website 2016)

In his 2012 report, Harwood refers to data gathered by Statistics Canada from the International Adult Literacy Survey to draw attention to the alarmingly weak level of literacy skills (reading, writing, oral communication) of thousands of Canadians who finished high school but have not attained the base levels of literacy they need. Harwood (2012, 3) reported that a level-3 literacy skill on the IALS (on a scale of 5) is the average level needed to fully function in Canadian society, "yet 43% of all students leaving Canada's high schools still do so with Level 1 and 2 skills."

One could strongly advocate researching the use of the CLB and the NCLC in the literacy domain. They are developed in a way that targets language competence within a holistic literacy framework. To advance a national dialogue about improving the essential skills for an important part of the adult population, the use of nationally developed guidelines would be ideal: it would provide a platform that all stakeholders could agree upon. Again, the future outlook of the Benchmarks and the potential use for adult Canadians is great.

6. The CCLB's Potential Role for Other Languages in Canada

Besides French and English, other languages spoken, taught, and used in Canada could benefit from the expertise of the CCLB. With the *Multiculturalism Act* (Government of Canada 1988), languages of immigrants can be taught in schools. For these languages, which include Ukrainian, Spanish, German, Arabic, Urdu, and Tagalog, there are no standards for competency descriptions or for program development. They may not benefit from an official status like French and English, but school boards and communities do offer language-program support. Since it is left up to boards and local programs to develop and assess the language-learning process, the CCLB could play a guiding role in developing specific benchmarks for these languages. It is much needed and a number of stakeholders would benefit from it.

7. Final Remarks

The goal of this chapter is to share possibilities for expanding the national and international role that the CCLB can play with regard to language education. Twenty years after its creation, and with two versions of the CLB, and the NCLC, as well as the batteries of materials for supporting professional language education, the Centre has anchored itself as a leading agency in the field. It has built strong roots in excellence on many levels and on many layers. As a member of the board of directors, I came to appreciate the CCLB and the outstanding work it carries. The research opportunities are abundant across Canada, in every one of the fields I have mentioned above. However, to move forward to the next twenty years, serious discussions need to be carried out among stakeholders, both provincially and federally. Many institutions and agencies, namely CMEC, IRCC, the tri-council, provincial ministers of education, and higher education, need to unite behind a great intellectual Canadian product that has been developed by scholars from across Canada to serve Canada.

References

AlHamid, Sofyan, and Samira ElAtia. 2016. "La diversité de la langue française en milieu académique : des représentations linguistiques aux enjeux sociolinguistiques." *Journée du savoir de l'ACFAS*.

Blackledge, Adrian. 2009. "*As a Country We Do Expect*: The Further Extension of Language Testing Regimes in the United Kingdom." *Language Assessment Quarterly* 6:6–16.

De Jong, John, Matthew Lennig, Anne Kerkhoff, and Petra Poelmans. 2009. "Development of a Test of Spoken Dutch for Prospective Immigrants." *Language Assessment Quarterly* 6:41–60.

ElAtia, Samira. 2011. "Choosing Language Competence Descriptors for Language Assessment: Validity and Fairness Issues." *Synergies Europe* 6:165–175.

———. 2012. "A Minority within a Minority: Challenges and Implications for New Francophone Immigrants Learning English." *Embracing Challenges: Proceeding of the 11th METU International ELT Convention*, 78–92.

———. 2015. "Assessing Across the Disciplines: Online Formative Assessment in Bilingual Education." *Next Generation Assessment Conference*. Fairfax, Virginia.

Employment and Social Development Canada. 2016. *Program requirements.* Accessed March 10, 2016. www.esdc.gc.ca/en/foreign_workers/hire/caregiver/requirements.page

Government of Canada. 1988. *Canadian Multiculturalism Act.* Ottawa: S.R.C. 24 (4e suppl.). Accessed December 20, 2015. http://laws-lois.justice.gc.ca/PDF/C-18.7.pdf.

Harwood, Chris. 2012. *State of Literacy and Essential Skills Field.* Ottawa: Canadian Literacy and Learning Network.

Omaggio-Hadley, Alice. 1993. "Research in language learning: Principles, processes, and prospects." *ACTFL Foreign Language Education Series* 24:96–123. Lincolnwood, I.L.: National Textbook.

———. 2001. *Teaching Language in Context*, 3rd ed. Boston: Heinle & Heinle.

Pawlikowska-Smith, Grazyna. 2000. *Canadian Language Benchmarks 2000: English as a Second Langauge for Adults.* Ottawa: Centre for Canadian Language Benchmarks.

Saif, Shahrzad. 2013. "The language proficiency of international teaching assistants in Canadian universities: training, assessment, and screening." *Canadian Association of Applied Linguistics Annual Conference.* University of Victoria, Canada.

Saville, Nick. 2009. Language Assessment in the Management of International Migration: A Framework for Considering the Issues. *Language Assessment Quarterly* 6:17–29.

Watt, David L., and Deidre M. Lake. 2000. *Canadian Language Benchmarks-TOEFL research project: A comparison study of the Canadian Language Benchmarks assessment and the test of English as a foreign language.* Research report. Accessed March 10, 2016. http://files.eric.ed.gov.login.ezproxy.library.ualberta.ca/fulltext/ED456665.pdf.

Notes

1. Present at LTRC 2008 were Shahrzad Saif from Laval University, Janna Fox from Carlton University, Samira ElAtia from the University of Alberta, David Watt from the University of Calgary, Eunice Jung from the University of Toronto, Liying Cheng from the Queen's University, and Carolyn Turner from McGill University.
2. Instead of using CLB/NCLC throughout the document, I will be using "Benchmarks" to refer to both.
3. Around the world, many sets of competence descriptors are being developed, but for almost a decade now, the CEFR has dominated the field. Other examples of competence descriptors are the ACTFL guidelines widely used in the 1980s and 1990s, and the CLB. In this chapter, the CLB and the ACTFL are used as a point of comparison to the CEFR.

Contributors

Élissa Beaulieu has over fifteen years of experience in the field of French as a second language. Beaulieu has been NCLC Program and Partnerships manager at the Centre for Canadian Language Benchmarks (CCLB) since 2010, where she has provided leadership in training instructors teaching French as a second language to immigrants. She has also played an integral role in the development of language training, pedagogical resources, and placement and performance tests for newcomers living in minority francophone communities.

Monique Bournot-Trites is an Associate Professor in the Department of Language and Literacy Education at the University of British Columbia. She teaches second language methodology in the Teacher Education program, and courses in second language assessment, research methods, and reading foundations at the graduate level. In 2010, she developed a French M.Ed. cohort at UBC taught by Web conference for French teachers across Canada, for which she has been the academic supervisor. Recently, she has been the project lead for writing the Theoretical Language Framework for the Canadian Language Benchmarks. She is currently working on research with colleagues from UBC and the University of Toronto, comparing the reading skills of Anglophones and allophones in French immersion elementary school. Most of her research interests are in French immersion:

in particular, research on the acquisition and development of second language, content learning in an additional language, evaluation of languages, intercultural competence, the teaching of grammar, and learning disabilities. She did her Master's Degree (1986) in School Psychology at UBC, and the title of her thesis was "Bilingualism and Reasoning Ability." Her Ph.D. (1998) was in Educational Psychology at UBC; her Ph.D. dissertation was titled "Relationships between Cognitive and Linguistic Processes and Second Language Production in French Immersion." She taught in French immersion in grade 1 and grade 3 before becoming a faculty member at UBC.

Samira ElAtia, recipient of the McCalla professorship, is director of graduate studies and associate professor of language education and the director of graduate studies at the bilingual faculty, Faculté Saint-Jean, of the University of Alberta. She holds a Ph.D. from the University of Illinois at Urbana-Champaign. She specializes in language assessment and evaluation of competencies; her research interest focuses on issues of fairness in assessment. She is a member of the Board of Directors of the Centre for Canadian Language Benchmarks in Ottawa. She has served on expert boards of several international testing agencies: Educational Testing Services in the USA, Pearson Education in the UK, The International Baccalaureate Organization, Chambre du commerce et de l'industrie de Paris, and the Centre international des études pédagogiques of the Ministry of Education in France. Recently, she has been interested in the use of data mining techniques and learning analytics in educational research. Her latest book, *Data Mining and Learning Analytics in Educational Research*, has been published by Wiley&Blackwell (2016).

Eve Haque is Associate Professor in the Department of Languages, Literatures and Linguistics at York University in Toronto. Her research and teaching interests include language policy and ethnolinguistic nationalism, and immigrant language training regimes and multiculturalism. She has published in such journals as *TESOL Quarterly*; *Pedagogy*, and *Culture and Society*, as well as the *Journal of Multilingual and Multicultural Development*. She is also the author of *Multiculturalism within a Bilingual Framework: Language, Race and Belonging in Canada* (University of Toronto Press, 2012).

Monika Jezak has worked since 1996 at the Official Languages and Bilingualism Institute, where she presently acts as Assistant Director. She conducts research in areas of language policy and planning, multilingualism, adult immigrants' bi-literacy, adult immigrants' second language education, and sociolinguistics of immigration. She has almost thirty years of experience in teaching French as a second language within various settings, such as immersion classes, various adult immigrant programs, and university. She has over fifteen years' experience in training second language teachers. She participated in the development and administration of language tests as President of the French as a Second Language Ottawa-Carleton Contest and as Coordinator of the FSL Certification Tests at the University of Ottawa. She has provided expertise to UNESCO and, since 2009, has acted as an expert in language policy at the Centre for Canadian Language Benchmarks.

Morgan Le Thiec holds an M.A. in French as a foreign language and a Ph.D. in Linguistics. She is a lecturer at the Département de didactique des langues at the Université du Québec à Montréal. She is also a specialized consultant in French as a Second Language (FSL) for adult immigrants and in the training of FSL teachers. She participated in updating Quebec's scale of French competency levels of adult immigrants and in the creation of the French curriculum guidelines for adult immigrants in Quebec. For several years, she has collaborated with the Centre for Canadian Benchmarks, creating online resources and training for adult immigrants and their instructors in Canadian classrooms.

Enrica Piccardo is Associate Professor at OISE, University of Toronto, and at the Université Grenoble-Alpes, France. She has extensive experience in language teaching, teacher training, and second/foreign language education research. A CEFR specialist, she has been collaborating with European Institutions on international projects (the ECML in Graz, Austria, as project co-ordinator, and the Council of Europe as project member). Her monograph *From Communicative to Action-Oriented: A Research Pathway* (2014), available on line, is being used in teacher education in Canada and beyond. She is the principal investigator of two SSHRC-funded research projects, QualiCEFR and Linguistic and Cultural Diversity Reinvented (LINCDIRE), and of a Council of Europe–funded project, QualiMatrix. Her research focuses on emotions and creativity in language education, assessment and its role in the curriculum, plurilingualism, and teacher education. She has presented in many countries and published in different languages. Some recent articles include one in *TESOL Quarterly* (2013), a co-edited issue of *The Canadian Modern Language Review* (2015), and a book chapter, "The impact of the CEFR on Canada's linguistic plurality: a space for heritage languages?" in *Rethinking Heritage Language Education,* edited by Peter Pericles Trifonas and Themistoklis Aravossitas (Cambridge University Press, 2014).

Anne Senior has over twenty-five years of education, experience, and expertise in the fields of adult English as a Second Language (ESL) and French as a Second Language (FSL) education and training, federally, provincially, and privately. Anne is the president of ASTEC Inc., an Ottawa-based language and cross-culture consulting company. She acts as a specialist consultant for the Centre for Canadian Language Benchmarks and contributed to the revision of the *Canadian Language Benchmarks: English as a Second Language for Adult Learners* and the *Canadian Language Benchmarks: English as a Second Language for Adult Literacy Learners*. Anne also supports the implementation of the CLB as a national standard through tool development, training, research, and policy advice. She is a member of Immigration, Refugees, and Citizenship Canada's Newcomer Language Advisory Body, the Ottawa Local Immigration Partnership, and the language table of the Canadian Network of Agencies for Regulation.

Antonella Valeo is an Assistant Professor at York University, where she teaches graduate courses in applied linguistics and ESL to undergraduate students. Her research focuses on instructed second language acquisition, form-focused instruction, and language teacher education and development. She has consulted on the CLB validation project and other CLB-related initiatives.

Politics and Public Policy

Series editor: Linda Cardinal

The study of politics has been reignited, sparked by debate on globalization, renewed citizen claims and transformations of the welfare state. In this context, the study of political regimes, ideas and processes as well as that of public policy contribute to refreshing our understanding of the evolution of contemporary societies. Public policy is at the heart of political and state actions. It frames the course and objectives adopted by governments and steers citizen initiatives and collective actions. Political analysis is increasingly complex and dynamic, embracing ever more diverse political, social, economic, cultural and identity-related phenomena. The *Politics and Public Policy* series is an ideal forum in which to present titles that foster important discussion and debate in Canada and around the world.

Previous titles in this collection

Linda Cardinal et Sébastien Grammond, *Une tradition et un droit :
  le Sénat et la représentation de la francophonie canadienne*, 2017.
Hélène Knoerr, Alysse Weinberg et Aline Gohard-Radenkovic (dir.),
  L'immersion française à l'université : politiques et pédagogies, 2016.
E.-Martin Meunier (dir.), *Le Québec et ses mutations culturelles :
  six enjeux pour le devenir d'une société*, 2016.
Anne Gilbert, Luisa Veronis, Marc Brosseau et Brian Ray (dir.),
  La frontière au quotidien, 2014.

For a complete list of our titles in this series, see:
https://press.uottawa.ca/series/politics-public-policy-and-globalization/politics-and-public-policy.html

www.ingramcontent.com/pod-product-compliance
Lightning Source LLC
Chambersburg PA
CBHW061350300426
44116CB00011B/2071